Mackinac Island Cottage Cookbook

MARCIA DUNNIGAN & BARBARA TOMS

Artwork by Sharon Griffes Tarr

Touch-Down Books
Naples, Florida

Copyright © 2017 by Marcia Dunnigan
All rights reserved.

No part of this publication may be reproduced, distributed, or transmitted in any form or by any means, including photocopying, recording, digital scanning, or other electronic or mechanical methods, without the prior written permission of the publisher, except in the case of brief quotations embodied in critical reviews and certain other noncommercial uses permitted by copyright law.

For permission requests, please address
Touch-Down Books
P.O. Box 110687
Naples, Florida 34108

Published 2017 by Touch-Down Books
Printed in the United States of America

19 18 17 1 2 3 4

ISBN: 978-0-692-89517-7
Library of Congress Control Number: 2017942672

Mackinac Island Cottage Cookbook is a collection of favorite recipes which are not necessarily original.

*Good food and fine art -
    one nurtures the body, the other the soul.*

Mackinac Island

East Shore

MACKINAC ISLAND, MICHIGAN

Mackinac Island has always held an attraction for people. Native Americans were first, followed by explorers, missionaries, fur traders, soldiers, and tourists. The Island is located in Lake Huron east of the Mackinac Bridge.

People are drawn to this northern Michigan gem to be transported back in time. "The horse is king" on the Island and visitors move about by foot, bicycle, and horse-drawn carriages only. Visitors come to experience a bit of the past, a slower pace, and the innate beauty of this unique Island treasure.

There are many attractions, both natural and manmade. The bluffs overlook the busy harbor and the Straits of Mackinac. The impressive Grand Hotel is located on the West Bluff; Fort Mackinac is on the East. Both bluffs boast many beautiful old Victorian "cottages". Many were built in the late 1800's. These cottages are populated with summer residents.

The views on Mackinac range from peaceful to spectacular. Limestone formations include Arch Rock, Sugar Loaf Rock, and Skull Cave. Fort Mackinac, built by the British in 1780, is open to the public during the summer season. It contains museums and guides, dressed in the period uniforms, who inform visitors about its history and demonstrate cannon and musket firing. The harbor bustles with sailboats, yachts, ferry boats, and kayaks. It is not uncommon to see 1000-foot long Great Lakes freighters passing through the Straits of Mackinac daily on the way to their destination.

The downtown offers shopping, hotels, restaurants, and world-famous fudge. Nearly a million people visit each summer season. Many become captivated by Mackinac and return again and again.

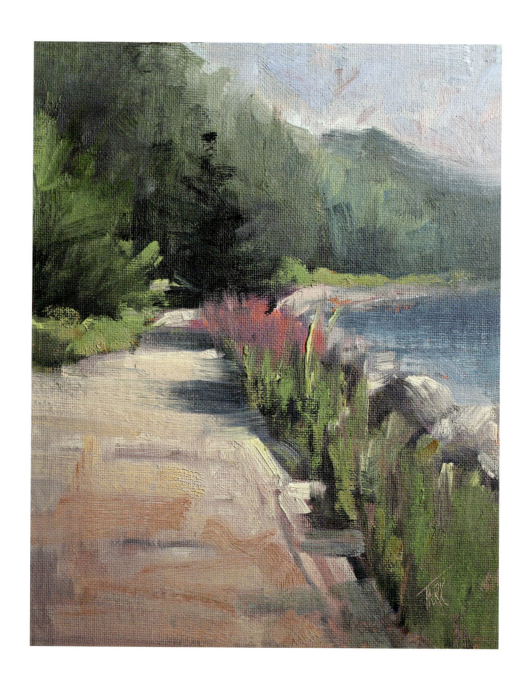

1 APPETIZERS

33 BREADS

43 BREAKFASTS

55 SOUPS

65 SALADS & DRESSINGS

85 BEEF & PORK

105 CHICKEN

121 FISH & SEAFOOD

133 PASTA

151 SIDE DISHES

173 DESSERTS

203 COOKIES

227 INDEX

APPETIZERS

Every summer the cottage fills up with family and friends and we love to spend time with them in various ways, especially over a beverage and some delicious homemade snacks in the late afternoon. Porch sitting at its best!

APPETIZER PIE
ARTICHOKE DIP
ARTICHOKE DIP – FLORENTINE
ARTICHOKE & SPINACH DIP
ARTICHOKE & CHEESE SPREAD
BAKED APRICOT SPREAD
BAGUETTE TOASTS
BLUE CHEESE DIP
BRIE APPETIZER
CRANBERRY RUM BRIE
BRIE WITH STRAWBERRY JAM
CHERYL'S BAKED BRIE
CHEESE - SAUSAGE BITES
CHEESY CORN BITES
CHICKEN SALAD TEA SANDWICHES
CHILI CON QUESO
CHILI PIMIENTO CHEESE SPREAD
CHILI-CRANBERRY MEATBALLS
CLAM DIP
CURRY DIP
DIANE'S DILL BITS
EASY CRAB SPREAD
FETA SALSA
FINGER JELL-O

GUACAMOLE DIP
HAM & CHEESE ROLL-UPS
HERB-COATED MOZZARELLA
HOT BEAN DIP
HOT CRAB DIP
JEANNE'S AVOCADO DIP
JEB'S FAVORITE SHRIMP DIP
MEXICAN FUDGE
MEX-TEX REFRIED BEANS DIP
MINI HAM & CHEESE SANDWICHES
MINI TURKEY SANDWICHES
MOCK BOURSIN CHEESE
MUSHROOMS
MUSTARD DIP
ONION RYE APPETIZERS
PIMIENTO CHEESE BALL
PINWHEELS
ROKA CHEESE ROLL
ROQUEFORT GRAPES
SEVEN-LAYER FIESTA DIP
SMOKED SALMON ROLL-UPS
SMOKED WHITEFISH SPREAD
SOUTHWEST SHRIMP DIP IN LETTUCE BOWL

SPINACH ROLL-UPS

SRIRACHA WINGS

STUFFED CELERY

STUFFED DATES

TACO APPETIZER

TACO DIP

THREE-LAYER CHEESE TORTE

VEGETABLE CHEESE DIP

VEGGIE DIP

VEGGIE PIZZA

WONTON WRAPPERS WITH SALAMI

APPETIZER PIE

8 ounces cream cheese, softened
2 tablespoons milk
1 (2-1/2 ounce) jar sliced dried beef, rinsed, dried, and finely chopped
1/8 teaspoon pepper
2 tablespoons instant minced onion
2 tablespoons green pepper, finely chopped
1/2 cup sour cream
1/4 cup chopped walnuts.

Blend cream cheese and milk; stir in beef, pepper, onion, and green pepper. Stir in sour cream. Place in small baking dish, sprinkle with walnuts. Bake at 350° for 15 minutes. Serve warm with crackers.

ARTICHOKE DIP – *Quick and Easy*

1 cup mayonnaise
1 (13 ounce) can artichoke hearts, drained and chopped
1 cup grated Parmesan cheese
Garlic salt to taste

Mix all ingredients together and pour into small oven-proof serving dish. Bake at 350° for 25 minutes. Serve warm with crackers or baguette toasts.

We have used light mayonnaise with great success!

Spinach fans rejoice! You'll love the next two recipes!

ARTICHOKE DIP – FLORENTINE

- 1 (10 ounce) package frozen chopped spinach, thawed and drained - press with paper towel to remove moisture
- 1 (13 ounce) jar marinated artichoke hearts, drained and chopped
- 12 ounces cream cheese, softened
- 1 cup freshly shredded Parmesan cheese
- 1/2 cup mayonnaise
- 3 large garlic cloves, pressed
- 2 tablespoons lemon juice
- 1-1/2 cups French breadcrumbs
- 2 tablespoons butter, melted

Combine all but crumbs and butter, stirring well. Spoon into lightly greased 11x7 baking dish. To make breadcrumbs, tear off a piece of baguette and place in food processor until coarse crumbs form. Combine crumbs and butter, sprinkle over spinach mixture. Bake uncovered at 375° for 25 minutes. Makes 4 cups. Serve with garlic bagel chips or crackers of your choice.

ARTICHOKE & SPINACH DIP

- 1 (13 ounce) can artichokes, chopped
- 1 (10 ounce) package frozen chopped spinach, well drained
- 8 ounces light cream cheese, softened
- 8 ounces Velveeta cheese

Mix together all ingredients until well blended. Heat in microwave until warm. Serve with your choice of raw vegetables or chips for dipping.

I continue to learn from my mother who is a wealth of wisdom and inspiration. She is always sharing time-saving tips with me so, together, we manage to serve wonderful meals and spend the least amount of time preparing! Thanks, Mom!

ARTICHOKE & CHEESE SPREAD

1 (14 ounce) can artichoke hearts, drained and chopped
1 cup mayonnaise
1/2 cup grated Parmesan cheese
4 ounces shredded Swiss cheese
1 teaspoon lemon juice
1/4 teaspoon salt
1/4 teaspoon pepper

Mix all ingredients until well blended and place in a buttered, small baking dish. Cover with foil. Bake at 300° for 40 minutes. Serve warm with crackers.

BAKED APRICOT SPREAD

8 ounces cream cheese, softened
1 cup shredded cheddar cheese
1/2 cup sour cream
1/2 cup dried apricots, chopped
1/3 cup sliced almonds

Mix cheeses until well blended. Add sour cream and apricots. Spread into 9-inch pie plate; sprinkle with almonds. Bake 25-30 minutes at 350° until almonds are lightly toasted and spread is heated through. Cool slightly. Serve with crackers.

BAGUETTE TOASTS – *Easy and Delicious!*

Cut baguette into thin (about 1/4 inch) slices. Place on baking sheet, brush with olive oil, sprinkle with salt and pepper, and bake for about 10 minutes at 350°. Cool and serve with any appetizer.

BLUE CHEESE DIP

8 slices bacon, diced
2 cloves garlic, minced
8 ounces cream cheese, softened
1/4 cup heavy cream
4 ounces crumbled blue cheese
2 tablespoons fresh chives, chopped
2 tablespoons almonds, chopped

Preheat oven to 350°. Cook bacon over medium-high heat until nearly crisp. Drain bacon and wipe skillet dry. Return bacon to pan, add garlic, and cook over medium heat until bacon is crisp. Make sure garlic doesn't burn. Drain on paper towels. Beat cream cheese in bowl until smooth. Add cream; beat well to mix. Fold in bacon, garlic, blue cheese, and chives. Transfer to a 2-cup baking dish; top evenly with almonds. Bake about 30 minutes or until heated through.

We usually serve trimmed vegetables, crackers, or baguette toasts with this dip. If you like blue cheese, this is sure to become one of your favorite appetizers!

BRIE APPETIZER

1 sheet frozen puff pastry
1 tablespoon unsalted butter
1/2 cup walnuts or pecans
1/8 teaspoon cinnamon
1 (8 ounces) Brie
1/4 cup brown sugar
1 egg, well beaten

Defrost pastry for about 20 minutes and unfold. Preheat oven to 375°. In saucepan, melt butter over medium heat. Sauté the nuts in the butter until golden brown, approximately five minutes. Add the cinnamon, stirring until nuts are well coated. Place mixture on top of the Brie and sprinkle brown sugar over the mixture. Place Brie in center of pastry. Press pastry around the Brie, folding and securing at the top. May use toothpicks to help secure. Brush top lightly with egg. Bake for 20 minutes until pastry is golden brown.

CRANBERRY RUM BRIE

1/2 cup canned whole cranberry sauce
1 tablespoon brown sugar
1/2 teaspoon imitation rum extract
1/8 teaspoon nutmeg, ground
8 ounces Brie cheese, room temperature
2 tablespoons pecans, chopped

Preheat oven to 450°. Mix cranberry sauce, sugar, extract, and nutmeg. Peel off top rind of Brie. Leave bottom and sides. Place in ovenproof dish. Top with cranberry mixture and sprinkle with pecans. Bake five to seven minutes until cheese softens. Serve with crackers or baguette toasts.

Although we serve sliced fresh apples with Brie, we highly recommend adding crackers and baguette toasts to the plate as well.

BRIE WITH STRAWBERRY JAM

1 (six-inch) wheel Brie cheese
3 tablespoons strawberry jam
2 teaspoon balsamic vinegar
1 cup strawberries, chopped
1/2 cup pecans, chopped
1/2 cup fresh mint leaves, chopped

Preheat oven to 275°. Place Brie on oven-safe dish. Cook jam and vinegar in small pan over medium heat until bubbly. Place chopped strawberries and pecans on top of Brie wheel. Cover with the jam mixture and bake until it is warm and soft, about fifteen minutes. Garnish with mint leaves. Serve immediately.

CHERYL'S BAKED BRIE

1/4 cup packed brown sugar
1/4 cup chopped pecans
1 tablespoon brandy
1 14-ounce round Brie

Mix brown sugar, pecans, and brandy in a small bowl. Refrigerate for at least least 12 hours. Preheat oven to 500°. Place the Brie in an oven proof serving dish and bake for four minutes, just enough to soften the cheese. Spread the sugar mixture evenly on top of the warm Brie and bake until the sugar melts, approximately two minutes.

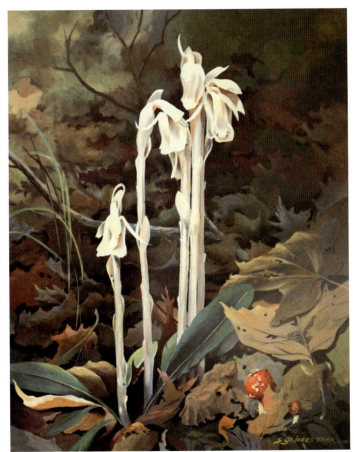

CHEESE - SAUSAGE BITES

1 pound extra sharp cheddar cheese, grated, room temperature
1 pound mild pork sausage
3 cups Bisquick buttermilk mix
2 eggs

Mix the cheese, sausage, Bisquick, and eggs. With your hands, shape into small balls and place about 1-1/4 inches apart on a baking sheet. Bake at 400° until just beginning to brown (12 to 15 minutes). Serve warm or cool and toss into freezer bags to freeze.

If frozen, thaw and then warm in oven at 350° before serving.

CHEESY CORN BITES

9 ounces cream cheese at room temperature
1 cup shredded pepper jack cheese
1 large egg
1/4 cup canned corn kernels
1 (10-ounce) bag scoop-shaped tortilla chips
Chopped chives or cilantro, for sprinkling

Preheat oven to 350° degrees. In large bowl, mix cream cheese, pepper jack cheese, egg, and corn. Arrange chips on large baking sheet and place one teaspoon corn mixture in each. Bake until filling sets, about 20 minutes. Sprinkle corn bites with chives; serve warm.

CHICKEN SALAD TEA SANDWICHES

3 cups chicken broth
2 whole chicken breasts, boneless with skin (about 1-1/2 pounds) halved
1 cup light mayonnaise
1/3 cup sweet onion, chopped very fine
1 teaspoon fresh tarragon leaves, minced
Salt and pepper to taste
24 sandwich bread slices with crusts removed
1/2 cup pecans, roasted and salted, finely chopped

Bring broth to a boil in a large skillet and add chicken breasts. Reduce heat to a low simmer. Cook, turning chicken once, for 7 minutes. Cool chicken in cooking liquid. Discard skin and finely chop or shred chicken. In a bowl, stir together chicken, 1/2 cup of mayonnaise, onion, tarragon, salt, and pepper. Make sandwiches and cut into quarters. Place pecans on a flat plate. Spread edges of sandwiches with remaining mayonnaise to coat well, and dip edges in pecans. May be made two hours ahead, wrapped in plastic wrap, and chilled.

Mom's tip: When we are short on time, we use canned chicken breasts. The sandwiches still seem to disappear from the platter!

CHILI CON QUESO

3/4 cup onion, chopped
1 tablespoon oil
1 (14.5 ounce) can diced tomatoes
1 (4-ounce) can chopped green chilies
3 cups shredded cheddar/jack cheese

Sauté onion in oil until tender. Do not brown. Drain tomatoes reserving liquid. Add tomatoes and chilies to onions. Simmer about 10 minutes. Stir in cheese till blended. If mixture needs diluting, add some of the reserved tomato liquid. **Don't forget tortilla chips!**

Appetizers | 11

CHILI PIMIENTO CHEESE SPREAD

8 ounces cream cheese, softened
1/2 cup mayonnaise
2 garlic cloves, minced
2 teaspoons sweet pickle relish, drained
4 cups shredded sharp cheddar
2 (4 ounce) cans diced pimiento, drained
1 (4 ounce) can chopped green chilies
1/2 cup chopped pecans, toasted

Combine cream cheese, mayonnaise, garlic, and pickle relish. Beat at medium speed with an electric mixer until smooth. Stir in cheddar cheese, pimiento, and green chilies. Place in a serving bowl and cover with the pecans. Cover and chill up to eight hours. Serve with pita chips, crackers, or vegetables. Makes 3 cups.

CHILI-CRANBERRY MEATBALLS

1 (5 pound) package meat balls
1 (13 ounce) can whole cranberry sauce
1 (12 ounce) jar chili sauce
1/2 cup brown sugar
1 tablespoon lemon juice

Mix last four ingredients and pour over meatballs. Bake for two hours at 250°. May also be prepared in a slow cooker. Serve warm.

CLAM DIP

1 (8 ounce) can minced clams
8 ounces cream cheese, softened
1 tablespoon lemon juice
1 tablespoon grated onion
1 teaspoon chopped parsley
1 teaspoon Worcestershire sauce
1/4 teaspoon salt
3 drops liquid hot pepper sauce

Drain clams and reserve liquid. Cream the cheese and add seasonings and clams. Mix thoroughly. Chill at least one hour. If necessary, use clam liquid to thin.

CURRY DIP

1 cup Hellmann's mayonnaise
1 teaspoon tarragon vinegar
1 teaspoon grated onion
1 teaspoon horseradish
1 teaspoon curry powder

Mix in blender and let ripen for a day or overnight in refrigerator. Serve with raw vegetables or cold shrimp. Makes one cup.

DIANE'S DILL BITS

4 ounces butter
6 ounces Rice Chex cereal
3 ounces Parmesan cheese
3 teaspoons dill weed
1/4 teaspoon salt

Melt butter in large heavy skillet. Add cereal and stir to light brown. Remove from heat and sprinkle combined cheese, dill weed, and salt over the cereal. Toss with fork to coat. Cool. Store air tight.

EASY CRAB SPREAD

Imitation crab, chopped fine
Mayonnaise
Dill Weed

Use any amount to your taste. Mom and I find that using a 1-pound package of the imitation crab makes plenty for a group of six or eight. We add the mayonnaise to make a nice spreading consistency and enough dill weed to give it great flavor.
Makes approximately 2 cups.

Although this is a good spread for crackers, we also use it as a filling for tea sandwiches.

FETA SALSA

1 (14.5 ounce) can tomatoes, drained, chopped
4 ounces crumbled feta cheese
1/4 cup sliced pitted ripe olives or Kalamata olives
3 tablespoons fresh basil, chopped
2 tablespoons green onions, chopped
1 tablespoon fresh lime juice
1 teaspoon dried oregano leaves

Mix all until well blended and serve with pita chips.

FINGER JELL-O

3 (3 ounce) Jell-O brand Gelatin (any flavor)
4 envelopes Knox Unflavored Gelatin
4 cups boiling water

Finger Jell-O is a favorite treat for everyone, from toddlers to grandparents! It's perfect to have on hand for any gathering of friends and family.

Mix gelatin packets and Knox unflavored gelatin together. (Jell-O packets may be of any flavor you want as long as the flavor is the same.) Pour boiling water in slowly while stirring. Stir completely until the mixture is fully dissolved. Pour into a pan that is roughly 13x9. Let the substance cool gradually for 30 minutes. Refrigerate for an additional hour or until it becomes firm. Cut in squares or with small cookie cutters for special designs.

GUACAMOLE DIP

1 large ripe avocado, peeled
2 teaspoons lemon or lime juice
2 teaspoons grated onion
1 ripe tomato, diced

Mash all ingredients together and chill. Serve with tortilla or corn chips.

HAM & CHEESE ROLL-UPS

3 ounces cream cheese
1 tablespoon mayonnaise
1/2 teaspoon prepared mustard
1/3 cup stuffed olives, chopped
1/4 teaspoon paprika
1/4 teaspoon onion powder
4 thin slices boiled ham

Mix all ingredients except ham together until well blended. Spread mixture on the ham slices, roll up (long edge), insert toothpicks about one-inch apart, and then slice between toothpicks for a bite size treat. Makes about twenty-four.

HERB-COATED MOZZARELLA

Dip mozzarella balls in olive oil and roll in a variety of fresh minced herbs such as chives, Italian parsley, basil, or dill. Fasten together a mozzarella ball and a cherry tomato with a toothpick and place on a serving platter.

HOT BEAN DIP

1 (32 ounce) can pinto beans, rinsed and drained
1/2 cup chicken broth
1 (10 ounce) can diced tomatoes with green chilies, drained and divided
1/2 teaspoon salt
1/4 teaspoon ground black pepper
1/4 teaspoon ground cumin
3/4 cup shredded sharp cheddar cheese

Blend half of the beans with chicken broth in food processor until smooth. Stir in remaining beans, 1 cup tomatoes, salt, pepper, and cumin. Spoon mixture into a lightly greased 1-1/2-quart baking dish. Top with cheddar cheese. Bake at 350° for 20 minutes until golden and bubbly. Top with remaining tomatoes and green chilies. Serve with tortilla chips.

HOT CRAB DIP

8 ounces cream cheese, softened
1 cup mayonnaise
1 envelope Hidden Valley Ranch Buttermilk Dressing Mix
2 tablespoons lemon juice
1 heaping tablespoon diced green chilies
1 large tomato, seeded and chopped
1/2 cup green onions, chopped
6 ounces fresh or canned crabmeat
Paprika

Preheat oven to 350°. In medium bowl, blend cream cheese, mayonnaise, salad dressing mix, and lemon juice until smooth. Stir in chilies, tomato, green onions, and crabmeat. Spoon mixture into small casserole dish. Bake for 15 minutes. Lightly dust with paprika. Serve immediately with fresh bread or crackers.

JEANNE'S AVOCADO DIP - *A Touch of Florida*

Jeanne warns that this may be addictive. She's right!

1 red onion, chopped very small
2 avocados, or 1 large Florida avocado, chopped small
1 (13 ounce) can black beans (drained and rinsed)
1 (10 ounce) can shoe peg corn (drained)
9 Roma tomatoes, seeded and cut small
Fresh cilantro, chopped, add to taste
1/4 to 1/2 bottle Paul Newman's Parmesan and Roasted Garlic Dressing

Stir all ingredients together, place in a bowl, and serve with your favorite chips.

JEB'S FAVORITE SHRIMP DIP

This recipe was shared in an article about Jeb Bush when he was Governor of Florida.

4 ounces sour cream
8 ounces cream cheese
1/2 cup celery, chopped
1/2 cup onion, chopped
Salt and pepper to taste
Red pepper to taste
Juice of one lemon
1 cup salad shrimp, chopped

Blend sour cream and cream cheese. Fold in celery and onion. Add salt, peppers, and lemon juice. Fold in shrimp. Serve with crackers or toast rounds.

MEXICAN FUDGE

8 ounces shredded cheddar cheese
8 ounces shredded Monterey Jack cheese
1/2 cup salsa, medium
3 eggs

Combine cheeses in a bowl. Beat eggs and salsa in small bowl. Put half of the cheese mixture in 8X8 pan. Pour salsa and egg mixture over cheese. Top with remaining cheese. Bake at 350° for 25 minutes. Cool slightly, cut into squares, place on a platter, and serve with tortilla chips. May also be prepared in a microwave on high until set.

Mexican fudge is so quick and easy to make! We keep it on the top of our "go-to" list and make it whenever a last-minute hors d'oeuvre is needed.

MEX-TEX REFRIED BEAN DIP

4 ounces cream cheese
1 cup sour cream
1/2 package taco seasoning mix
1 (16 ounce) can refried beans
1 bunch green onions, chopped
1 (8 ounce) package sharp cheddar cheese, shredded

Blend cream cheese, sour cream, and taco mix. Add refried beans and mix until well blended. Stir in green onions and about 6-ounces of the cheddar cheese. Spread in a greased baking dish and sprinkle remaining cheese on top. Bake for 20 to 30 minutes at 350° until hot and cheese is lightly browned. Serve with tortilla chips.

MINI HAM & CHEESE SANDWICHES

2 packages Pepperidge Farm mini-dinner rolls
1/2 pound shaved ham
1/2 pound Swiss cheese slices
1/2 pound butter
2 tablespoons dark brown sugar
2 tablespoons Worcestershire sauce
1 tablespoon mustard
2 tablespoons poppy seed

Slice the package of dinner rolls lengthwise. Do not separate rolls. Layer the ham and cheese on bottom half and cover with top half. Mix melted butter with remaining ingredients. Pour over sandwiches and bake uncovered at 350° for about 30 minutes until brown and mushy. (If larger rolls are used, slice lengthwise in thirds and discard centers.) Easy to freeze. Prepare sandwiches completely but do not bake until ready to serve.

MINI TURKEY SANDWICHES

1 cup mayonnaise
2 tablespoons apricot preserves
1 tablespoon Dijon mustard
2 (12 ounce) packages dinner rolls
1 pound smoked turkey
1 Granny Smith apple, chopped
12 slices provolone cheese
1 tablespoon butter, melted
Sesame seeds
Dried minced onion

Preheat oven to 350°. Combine mayonnaise, preserves, and mustard in a small bowl. Without separating dinner rolls, cut in half lengthwise. Spread mayonnaise mixture on cut sides. Layer turkey, apple, and cheese over bottom half of prepared rolls. Cover with top half of prepared rolls. Place on baking sheet and brush tops with melted butter. Sprinkle tops with sesame seeds and dried minced onion. Bake ten minutes or until cheese is melted. Cut into individual sandwiches.

MOCK BOURSIN CHEESE

2 (8 ounce) packages cream cheese
1/2 teaspoon basil leaves
2 tablespoons whipping cream
1/2 teaspoon dried dill weed
1 clove garlic, crushed
1/2 teaspoon caraway seeds
Lemon pepper

Cream all ingredients, except lemon pepper, together. Cover well and refrigerate Before serving, sprinkle the top with lemon pepper. Serve on crackers.

MUSHROOMS

3 pounds mushrooms
1 teaspoon pepper
1 pound butter
1 teaspoon minced garlic
1 quart Burgundy
2 cups boiling water
1-1/2 tablespoons Worcestershire sauce
4 beef bouillon cubes
4 chicken bouillon cubes
1 teaspoon dill weed

Combine all ingredients. Cover and cook on stove top until boiling. Reduce heat to low and simmer for six hours. Serve warm using appetizer forks or toothpicks.

MUSTARD DIP

1/4 cup dry mustard
1 cup (scant) apple cider vinegar
2 eggs
1 cup sugar

Stir together mustard and vinegar in the top of a double boiler. Let sit for four hours or overnight. Mix eggs and sugar. Stir into the mustard mix and cook over a double boiler for about an hour or a bit longer, until thick, stirring occasionally. Let cool. Mustard dip keeps well in refrigerator.

This mustard dip is so easy to make and it's a winner with both crisp, hard pretzels and soft, homemade pretzels. We started making this mustard and the soft pretzels about ten years ago when our adult "kids" wanted the perfect snack to go with a cold Michigan beer. Time to break out the cribbage board and croquet set!

ONION RYE APPETIZERS

2 (8 ounce) cans French-fried onions, crushed
3/4 cup cooked bacon, crumbled
1/2 cup mayonnaise or salad dressing
3 cups shredded Swiss cheese
1 (16 ounce) package snack rye bread
1 (14 ounce) jar pizza sauce

Combine onions, bacon, mayonnaise, and cheese. Spread about one teaspoon of pizza sauce on each slice of bread. Top with about one tablespoon of cheese mixture. Bake on an ungreased baking sheet at 350° for 12-14 minutes or until heated through and cheese is melted. To freeze appetizer: cover and freeze in a single layer for up to two months. Bake as above for 14-16 minutes.

PIMIENTO CHEESE BALL

8 ounces cream cheese, softened
1/3 cup parsley, finely chopped
1/2 cup sour cream
1/4 cup butter, softened
2 tablespoons pimiento, finely chopped
1 tablespoon onion, grated
1/3 cup chopped nuts
1 tablespoon parsley

Combine and mix until well blended all ingredients except nuts and parsley. Shape into ball or log. Coat with nuts and parsley and serve with assorted crackers.

PINWHEELS

16 ounces cream cheese, softened
1 envelope Hidden Valley Original Ranch Salad Dressing & Seasoning Mix
2 green onions, minced
4 (12-inch) flour tortillas
1 (4 ounce) can diced pimientos, rinsed and drained
1 (4 ounce) can diced chilies, rinsed and drained
2-1/3 ounces sliced ripe olives, rinsed and drained

Mix cream cheese, dressing mix, and onions until blended. Spread on tortillas. Blot dry the pimientos, chilies, and olives on paper towels. Sprinkle equal amounts of each over cream cheese mixture. Roll tightly and cover in cling wrap. Chill at least two hours. Cut rolls into one-inch pieces. Discard ends. **So good, so easy, and beautiful to serve.**

ROKA CHEESE ROLL

8 ounces cream cheese, softened
1 (5 ounce) jar Kraft ROKA Blue Spread
1/2 teaspoon garlic powder
3/4 cup chopped pecans
1/4 cup dried cranberries

Mix cheeses and garlic powder until well blended. Refrigerate for two hours. Shape into ball and coat with pecans and cranberries. Serve with crackers.

ROQUEFORT GRAPES

1 (10 ounce) package almonds, pecans, or walnuts, toasted
8 ounces cream cheese, softened
2 ounces Roquefort cheese, softened
2 tablespoons heavy cream
1 pound seedless grapes (red or green), washed and dried

To toast nuts: Preheat oven to 275°. Spread nuts on baking sheet and bake until toasted, about eight minutes, turning half way through. Almonds should be light golden brown; pecans & walnuts should smell toasted, not burned. Chop toasted nuts coarsely and spread on platter. Beat cream cheese, Roquefort, and cream until smooth. Drop grapes into mixture and stir by hand to coat them. Roll coated grapes in toasted nuts and place on a tray lined with waxed paper. Chill until ready to serve. Any leftover cheese mixture may be frozen and used at a later date.

SEVEN-LAYER FIESTA DIP

1 (16 ounce) can refried beans
16 ounces sour cream
1 envelope taco seasoning mix
8 ounces shredded cheddar cheese
1 cup prepared guacamole
1 cup fresh tomatoes, chopped
1/2 cup green onions, sliced
1/2 cup black olives, sliced

Spread refried beans in shallow serving dish. Mix sour cream and seasoning mix in small bowl until well blended. Spread over refried beans. Top with layers of remaining ingredients. Serve with tortilla chips.

SMOKED SALMON ROLL-UPS

8 ounces cream cheese, softened
1/4 cup feta cheese
4 (10-inch) flour tortillas (may use spinach-flavored)
1 (3-1/2 ounce) jar capers
1/4 cup onions, finely chopped
8 ounces smoked salmon, thinly sliced
1 cup baby spinach leaves

The colors of the salmon and the greens are beautiful in the roll-ups.

Mix cheeses until well blended. Spread cheese on tortillas; top with capers, onions, salmon, and spinach. Tightly roll up tortillas and wrap in plastic wrap. Refrigerate at least 2 hours or overnight. Cut each roll-up into 12 pieces.

SMOKED WHITEFISH SPREAD

8 ounces cream cheese, softened
1/2 pound smoked whitefish, skinned, boned and flaked
2 tablespoons green onions, finely chopped
1 tablespoon fresh dill, chopped
1 teaspoon lemon juice
1/4 teaspoon freshly ground pepper

Mix all until well blended. Cover and refrigerate for 3 hours. Makes about 1-1/2 cups. Serve with crackers.

SOUTHWESTERN SHRIMP DIP IN LETTUCE BOWL

1 iceberg lettuce
1 pound cooked salad shrimp, rinsed and drained
1/2 cup red bell pepper, finely chopped
1/2 cup salsa (hot)
1/2 cup canned corn, drained
1/2 cup green onions, chopped
2 tablespoons fresh parsley, chopped
1/2 cup mayonnaise
1/3 cup sour cream
1/2 teaspoon lemon juice

Take out core and trim one-inch-slice from the core end of lettuce head. Take out center, leaving 1/2-inch-thick shell. Wrap in moist paper towel to chill. Mix all other ingredients in bowl and chill for at least 1 hour. Place lettuce bowl on a platter. Spoon shrimp dip into the bowl. To serve, arrange veggies, baguette toasts, and crackers around lettuce bowl.

The lettuce bowl filled with the colorful shrimp mixture looks very pretty on the appetizer table. And, to top it off, it's delicious!

SPINACH ROLL-UPS

1 (10 ounce) package frozen chopped spinach, thawed and well drained
1 cup mayonnaise
8 ounces sour cream
1 bunch green onions, chopped
1 envelope ranch-style dressing mix
1 (3 ounce) jar bacon bits
9 (10-inch) flour tortillas

Mix together all ingredients except tortillas. Spread evenly on tortillas and roll up, pressing edges to seal, and wrap in plastic wrap. Chill 4 to 6 hours. Cut into 1/2-inch thick slices. Makes 6 dozen. You may freeze roll-ups. Cut in slices just before serving.

SRIRACHA WINGS – *Eric's best!*

3 pounds chicken wings, separated
Baking powder
Salt
Pepper
Emeril seasonings
Juice of one lime juice
4 ounces butter, melted
2 to 3 tablespoons Sriracha
1 clove garlic, minced and gently sautéed

Dry wings and sprinkle with baking powder. Let stand for 20 minutes. Preheat oven to 425°. Season wings with salt, pepper, and Emeril seasonings. Place on baking sheet lined with parchment paper. Bake for about 45 to 50 minutes until crisp. Turn wings every 10 to 15 minutes. When crisp, remove wings from oven and dip in mixture of butter, lime, garlic, and Sriracha Sauce. Serve with celery, ranch dressing, and blue cheese dressing.

Sriracha sauce is becoming quite popular and can be found in most grocery stores. It is a hot sauce made from chili peppers, garlic, vinegar, salt, and pepper.

STUFFED CELERY

Small can crabmeat
Small can water chestnuts
1 teaspoon Worcestershire sauce
1 tablespoon lemon juice
1 teaspoon soy sauce
Mayonnaise as needed
1 bunch celery, cut in about three-inch strips

Finely chop crabmeat and water chestnuts. Combine remaining ingredients to make a thick spread. Stuff celery stalks with mixture.

STUFFED DATES

3 ounces cream cheese, softened
3 ounces Gorgonzola cheese, crumbled
2 tablespoons orange juice
8 ounces pitted dates
36 walnut halves

In small bowl, blend the cheeses together until well blended. Stir in orange juice. Spoon mixture into a medium, sealable plastic bag. Squeeze mixture toward one corner of the bag; separate dates along slits. Squeeze about 1-teaspoon cheese mixture into cavity, top with walnut piece. May be made one day ahead. Cover and refrigerate. Serve at room temperature.

TACO APPETIZER

2 (8 ounce) packages cream cheese, softened
1 envelope taco seasoning
1 cup salsa
1 bunch green onions, chopped
2 tomatoes, chopped
1/2 cup black olives, sliced
1 cup shredded cheddar cheese
Tortilla chips

Blend until the cream cheese and taco seasoning until smooth. Place mixture in middle of plate, smoothing the middle and leaving a ridge on the edges. Top with salsa and layer the green onions, chopped tomatoes, black olives, and shredded cheddar cheese. Surround with tortilla chips.

TACO DIP

1 (15 ounce) can refried beans
1/2 envelope taco seasoning
1 small container of avocado dip
1/2 cup bunch green onions, chopped

8 ounces sour cream
1 (15 ounce) pitted black olives, cut up
2 tomatoes, cut very small
3/4 cup shredded Monterey Jack cheese

Mix beans and taco seasoning together. Spread on the bottom of a serving dish. Follow with layers of the remaining ingredients in the order listed. Serve with tostados and enjoy!

THREE-LAYER CHEESE TORTE

- 3 (8 ounce) packages cream cheese, softened and divided
- 3 tablespoons pimiento-stuffed green olives, chopped
- 2 teaspoons olive juice
- 1 tablespoon mayonnaise
- 1 cup shredded sharp cheddar cheese
- 1 (2 ounce) jar diced pimiento, drained
- 1 teaspoon grated onion
- 1/4 cup butter
- 1 garlic clove, pressed
- 1 teaspoon dried Italian seasoning
- Parsley sprigs for garnish

Line 8x4-inch loaf pan on sides and bottom with plastic wrap.

<u>Layer 1:</u> Beat one package cream cheese at medium speed until creamy; stir in olives and olive juice. Spread mixture into bottom of loaf pan.

<u>Layer 2:</u> Beat one package cream cheese as above; add mayonnaise and cheddar cheese and beat until blended. Stir in pimiento and onion. Spread over first layer.

<u>Layer 3:</u> Beat one package cream cheese with butter as above; add garlic and Italian seasoning, beating until blended. Spread over second layer.

Cover and chill at least 3 hours or until firm. Invert on serving platter. Remove plastic wrap. Garnish with parsley. Serve with assorted crackers and grapes.

VEGETABLE CHEESE DIP

- 1/2 cup cream
- 1/2 teaspoon salt
- 12 ounces cottage cheese
- 3 ounces cream cheese, softened
- 1/2 pound sharp cheddar cheese, shredded

Mix cream, salt, and cottage cheese in blender until smooth.
Add cream cheese and cheddar cheese and blend. Serve with fresh raw vegetables.

VEGGIE DIP

8 ounces cream cheese, softened
8 ounces sour cream
1 tablespoon fresh thyme, chopped
2 teaspoons fresh rosemary, chopped
2 teaspoons lemon juice
1/2 teaspoon garlic powder
1/4 teaspoon seasoned salt

Beat cheese until creamy. Add remaining ingredients, beating well. Serve with fresh veggies.

VEGGIE PIZZA

2 cans crescent refrigerator rolls
8 ounces cream cheese
1 cup mayonnaise
1 envelope Hidden Valley Ranch dry mix
Miscellaneous mixed vegetables and sliced olives
Mozzarella cheese, shredded

Spread rolls on 11x15 baking sheet. Press together to seal seams. Bake at 375° approximately 12 minutes until light brown. Mix cream cheese, mayonnaise, and dressing mix together. Spread mix over crust. Top with finely chopped vegetables such as broccoli, cauliflower, green pepper, carrots, tomatoes, sliced olives. Top with mozzarella cheese. Cut in squares or bars. Refrigerate and serve with fresh vegetables.

WONTON WRAPPERS WITH SALAMI

Place salami slice on wrapper and roll up. Dip fingers in water and seal the wrapper. Bake on greased baking pan at 350° until golden brown and crispy. Serve with mustard. Wontons can also be used open-face. Spray a little oil on both sides of wrapper. Put cheese, pepperoni, and a small tomato slice on top and bake.

BREADS

There is something about bread that just seems to hit the spot at any time on any day, at least for our family. Even our dog, Sophie, has been known to grab a roll when no one is looking! We love our "bad dog"!

BEA'S MONDEL BREAD

CHERRY SWIRL COFFEE CAKE

CINNAMON ROLLS

MONKEY BREAD

ORANGE NUT BREAD

PULL-A-PART BREAD

PUMPKIN BREAD

QUICK CHEESE & GARLIC BREAD

SALTY BREAD STICKS

SIX-WEEKS BRAN MUFFINS

SOUR CREAM COFFEE CAKE

ZOMBIE BREAD

ZUCCHINI WALNUT BREAD

BEA'S MONDEL BREAD

1/2 cup oil
3/4 cup sugar
2 eggs
Dash of salt
1 teaspoon vanilla

2 cups flour
2 teaspoons baking powder
3 ounces chopped nuts
Cinnamon-sugar mix, 3/4-teaspoon cinnamon to 2-tablespoons sugar

Mix oil, sugar, eggs, salt, and vanilla with a mixer. Combine flour and baking powder. Add nuts and stir into egg mixture. Grease cookie sheet. Divide dough in half and form into two logs, each about 2-inches wide. Sprinkle top with sugar and cinnamon. Bake at 350° for 20 minutes. Remove from oven and immediately slice into 3/4-inch pieces. Lay slices on sides on cookie sheet, sprinkle with cinnamon-sugar mix, and brown for ten minutes. Turn and sprinkle with remaining cinnamon-sugar mix. Turn oven down to 250° and bake until golden and crispy.

CHERRY SWIRL COFFEE CAKE

1-1/2 cups sugar
1/2 cup butter, softened
1/2 cup shortening
1-1/2 teaspoons baking powder
1 teaspoon vanilla extract
1 teaspoon almond extract
4 eggs
3 cups flour
1 (21 ounce) can cherry pie filling
Glaze

Heat oven to 350°. Grease jelly-roll pan. Blend sugar, butter, shortening, baking powder, vanilla, almond extract, and eggs in bowl on low speed. Beat 3 minutes on high speed. (Do not overbeat). Stir in flour. Spread 2/3 of the batter in jelly-roll pan. Spread pie filling over batter. Drop remaining batter by tablespoon onto pie filling. Bake 45 minutes. While warm, drizzle with glaze (1 cup powdered sugar and 1-2 tablespoons milk).

CINNAMON ROLLS – *Margaret's finest!*

1 (2 loaves, 32 ounce) package frozen bread dough
1/2 cup melted butter
1/3 cup brown sugar
1/2 cup white sugar
2 teaspoons plus cinnamon
1/2 cup chopped nuts
1 cup powdered sugar
1-2 tablespoons milk

Thaw bread according to directions. Combine loaves and flatten. Separate evenly in eight pieces. Roll each on lightly floured board into a roll about 18-inches long. Brush with melted butter on both sides. Mix sugars and cinnamon together and sprinkle on cookie sheet. Roll bread in mixture and place on greased pizza pan forming into coil. Continue with each strip connecting ends and forming into one large coil. Sprinkle with nuts. Bake at 350° for 30-35 minutes. Prepare glaze by thoroughly mixing the powdered sugar and milk. Drizzle over the rolls.

MONKEY BREAD

12 frozen cinnamon rolls, thawed
3/4 cup sugar
1/3 cup butter, melted
1/2 cup caramel topping
1/2 cup chopped pecans

Thaw rolls, cut in quarters. Dip each quarter in butter and roll in sugar. Prepare Bundt pan and place rolled sections in the bottom. Sprinkle with the chopped pecans and drizzle with caramel topping. Cover with plastic wrap and let double in size. Remove wrap and bake at 350° for 35-40 minutes. Cool a minute or two and then turn out onto a serving plate. Serve warm and don't count on any leftovers!

ORANGE NUT BREAD

2-1/4 cups all purpose flour
2-1/2 teaspoons baking powder
1/4 teaspoon soda
3/4 teaspoon salt
3 tablespoons shortening
3/4 cup sugar
1 egg, beaten
3/4 cup orange juice
1/2 cup chopped nuts

Spray a 9x5x3-inch loaf pan well. Sift flour and measure. Add baking powder, soda, salt, and sift three more times. Cream shortening and sugar well, add egg and beat until smooth and fluffy. Add orange juice and sifted dry ingredients alternately in three portions, beating until smooth after each. Fold in nuts. Turn into prepared pan, cover with aluminum foil. Bake at 325° for 20 minutes, uncover and bake 50 minutes longer. Remove from pan and cool.

PULL-APART BREAD

1/2 to 3/4 cup nuts (optional)
3/4 cup sugar
2 teaspoons cinnamon
3 or 4 cans Pillsbury refrigerator biscuits
4 ounces butter, melted
1 cup brown sugar
1/4 teaspoon vanilla

Grease and flour Bundt pan and preheat oven to 350°. Sprinkle half of the nuts in bottom of pan. Mix sugar and cinnamon. Cut each biscuit in thirds and roll each in sugar mixture. Place half of the biscuits in pan and sprinkle remaining nuts over them. Place rest of biscuits in pan. Mix butter, brown sugar, vanilla, and remaining sugar mixture. Spoon over top and bake for 30 to 35 minutes. Remove bread from pan as soon as it comes out of the oven.
You will only have to call the gang to the table once to pull apart this warm, yummy treat!

We love to work in the garden, especially when dear friends and family pitch in. Everyone has ideas and suggestions as to where things should be planted. So, our gardens are truly an unprofessional work of love. The only exception being when our cousins, who are landscape architects, weigh in. We always listen to them!

Mackinac Island Cottage Cookbook

PUMPKIN BREAD

1 cup oil
3 cups sugar
4 eggs
2 cups canned pumpkin
2/3 cup water
3-1/2 cups flour
2 teaspoons baking soda
1-1/2 teaspoons salt
1 teaspoon nutmeg
1 teaspoon cinnamon

This easy to make, mild, and moist bread is an all-time family favorite. Mom and I like to make it into little cream-cheese sandwiches for Book Club or any special occasion with friends. We bake the bread in old-fashioned metal ice cube trays (without insets) which makes the perfect size for little tea sandwiches. Just cut loaf into slices, spread with cream cheese, top with second slice, and cut in half.

Heat oven to 350°. Grease two 9x5x3 loaf pans. In large bowl, cream shortening and sugar until fluffy. Stir in eggs, pumpkin, and water. Combine the flour, soda, salt, nutmeg, and cinnamon and gradually blend into the pumpkin mixture. Pour into pans and bake approximately 60 minutes or until wooden pick inserted comes out clean.

QUICK CHEESE & GARLIC BREAD

16 ounce loaf French bread
1/3 cup grated Parmesan cheese
1/2 cup butter, softened
2 tablespoons olive oil
2 tablespoons garlic powder
1 teaspoon dried parsley
1/2 teaspoon dried rosemary
1/2 teaspoon basil

Slice bread in half, length wise. Place Parmesan cheese, softened butter, olive oil, garlic powder, parsley, rosemary, and basil in a bowl. Mix thoroughly (I use a hand mixer) and spread on the bread. Place open-faced in 350° oven for 5 minutes. Then, broil for 5 minutes until browned on top. **Quick Cheese and Garlic Bread is an appealing addition to any meal, especially when serving soup or pasta.**

SALTY BREAD STICKS

1/4 cup butter
1-1/4 cups all-purpose flour
2 teaspoons sugar
2 teaspoons baking powder
1 teaspoon salt
2/3 cup milk
Coarse salt

Heat oven to 450°. Melt butter in a 9-inch square pan in oven. Remove as soon as butter melts. Stir together flour, sugar, baking powder, and 1 teaspoon salt. Add milk and mix with a fork until dough clings together. Knead lightly about 10 times on a floured surface. Roll 1/2 inch thick into an 8-inch square. Cut in half with a floured knife and then cut each half into 9 sticks, each 4 inches long. Dip in melted butter, place in square pan, and sprinkle with coarse salt. Bake 15 to 20 minutes and serve hot.

SIX-WEEKS BRAN MUFFINS – **thanks to Aunt Polly!**

1 (15-ounce) box raisin bran cereal
5 cups flour
2 teaspoons salt
5 teaspoons soda
3 cups sugar
4 eggs, beaten
1 cup vegetable oil
1 quart buttermilk

Consider keeping a container of this batter on hand. It's an easy way to have fresh, hot muffins on demand. With our active, hungry family, it's a great choice to keep everyone happy and ready for the next Island adventure.

Mix cereal, flour, salt, soda, and sugar in large bowl. Beat eggs, oil, and milk. Mix together with dry ingredients. Keep in refrigerator and bake as needed at 400° for 15 to 20 minutes in paper-lined muffin pans. This recipe lasts in refrigerator up to six weeks. **In truth, our batter has never lasted six weeks! The muffins are much too popular!**

SOUR CREAM COFFEE CAKE

2 cups sifted cake flour
1 teaspoon baking powder
1/4 teaspoon salt
1 cup butter
2 cups sugar
1/2 teaspoon vanilla
2 eggs
1 cup sour cream

<u>Topping</u>
1/2 cup brown sugar
1 teaspoon cinnamon
1/2 cup chopped nuts

This is so delicious that we not only make it at the cottage but also in the winter at home! We have been making it for Christmas breakfast and sharing it with friends since 1980. Mom and I agree that great baked goods are perfect any time of year. They are for special people, not just special occasions.

Sift dry ingredients together. Cream butter, sugar, and vanilla until light and fluffy. Add eggs and beat. Blend in sour cream. Add dry ingredients. Spread half of batter in greased angel food cake pan. Sprinkle half of the topping mixture over batter. Add remaining batter and then remaining topping. Bake at 350° for one hour. Cool and turn onto plate.

We think this is especially beautiful on one of my mother-in-law's stunning, antique cake plates.

Mom and I do our best to keep Sharon well-fed so that she has the energy to paint all day! We are inspired and awed by her talent and passion for sharing her gift. Mackinac Island is a veritable treasure trove of fabulous subject matter for artists. Be sure to look around you when you visit and you, too, will be able to take in the beauty of the Island.

ZOMBIE BREAD

1 pound grated sharp cheddar cheese
1/2 cup minced parsley
Juice of one lemon
1-1/2 teaspoon salt
1/4 teaspoon pepper
¼ teaspoon garlic powder
1/2 pound butter, melted
2 loaves French bread

Mix cheese, parsley, lemon juice, salt, pepper, and garlic powder. Beat in the melted butter to make a paste. (It can be refrigerated at this point until you are ready to use it, but bring to room temperature before using.) Cut French bread in half lengthwise. Cut each half of loaf at about two inch intervals being careful not to cut through the bottom crust. Spread cut surfaces with the cheese paste and let stand for two hours. Place on large cookie sheet and bake at 350° until cheese is slightly melted and browned.

ZUCCHINI WALNUT BREAD

4 eggs
2 cups sugar
1 cup vegetable oil
3-1/2 cups flour
1-1/2 teaspoons baking soda
1-1/2 teaspoons salt
1 teaspoon cinnamon
3/4 teaspoon baking powder
2 cups grated zucchini (do not peel)
1 cup raisins (optional)
1 cup walnuts, chopped (optional)
1 teaspoon vanilla
Powdered sugar (optional)
Cream (optional)

Beat eggs, gradually beat in sugar, then oil. Combine dry ingredients; add to first mixture alternately with zucchini. Stir in raisins, walnuts, and vanilla. Turn into two prepared loaf pans. Bake on lowest rack at 350° for about 55 minutes until loaves test done. Let stand about 10 minutes; turn out onto wire racks to cool. If desired, loaves may be lightly glazed with powdered sugar mixed to spreading consistency with a little cream.

Mom's tip: *This bread freezes well, so make it, freeze it, and have it on-hand for afternoon coffee or tea time.*

BREAKFASTS

Coffee, conversation, fellowship, and good food are hallmarks of a happy breakfast or brunch gathering. We welcome the morning chirping of birds, the clip-clop of horses, and the sounds from the wakening harbor to provide the perfect setting to launch a new day.

BACON, EGG, & TOMATO STRATA

BANANA CREAM CRUMBLE FRENCH TOAST

BASIC QUICHE

BREAKFAST CROCKPOT CASSEROLE

BREAKFAST MUFFINS

BRUNCH ENCHILADAS

BRUNCH FRUIT CUP

CHRIS'S EASY CHEESE SOUFFLÉ

GREEN CHILE BRUNCH BAKE

HOT FRUIT

HUEVOS RANCHERO

OVERNIGHT FRENCH TOAST CASSEROLE WITH STRAWBERRIES

SPINACH, BACON, & MUSHROOM QUICHE

THEO'S TOAST WITH AVACADO & FRESH TOMATO

TOMATO FLORENTINE QUICHE

VIVIAN'S COTTAGE CHEESE PANCAKES

BACON, EGG, & TOMATO STRATA – *Make it tonight, serve it tomorrow!*

- 4 slices bacon or turkey bacon
- 1 (10 ounce) package sliced fresh mushrooms
- 1 medium onion, thinly sliced
- 2 garlic cloves, minced
- 2 cups low-fat or skim milk
- 4 large eggs
- 2 egg whites
- 6 cups firm whole-wheat Italian bread, cut into 3/4-inch cubes
- 1-1/2 cups shredded extra-sharp cheddar cheese
- 1 cup grape or cherry tomatoes, halved

Cook bacon in a large nonstick skillet until crisp; cool and crumble. Discard all but two teaspoons of fat in the skillet. Add mushrooms, onion, and garlic. Sauté until soft, about ten minutes. Remove from the heat and let cool.

Beat together milk, eggs, and egg whites in a large bowl. Prepare a 9x13-inch baking dish with nonstick spray. Spread half of the bread cubes over the bottom and sprinkle with half of the cooled vegetable mixture and one-third of the cheese. Pour half of the milk-egg mixture over the vegetables and cheese.

Repeat layers, top evenly with the crumbled bacon and tomato halves, and sprinkle with remaining cheese. Pour remaining milk-egg mixture over the top and press down until bread pieces are soaked.

Lay a sheet of plastic wrap directly on the top surface of the casserole; refrigerate overnight. Preheat oven to 325°. Remove plastic wrap and cover the casserole with foil. Bake until puffy, about 45 minutes. Remove foil and continue baking until lightly browned along the edges, about 10-15 minutes more. Makes 8 servings.

BANANA CREAM CRUMBLE FRENCH TOAST

14-16 slices of French bread
8 eggs
1 cup cream
2 cups whole milk
1 teaspoon vanilla
1 mashed banana

Brown Sugar Crumble Mixture
2 cups brown sugar
1 cup oatmeal
1 cup grape nuts
1 (4 ounce) butter
1/2 cup molasses

Prepare 10x15-inch glass baking dish with baking spray. Place bread slices in dish. Beat together the eggs, cream, milk, vanilla, and banana. Pour over bread. Cover and refrigerate overnight. In the morning, remove baking dish from refrigerator and bring it to room temperature. Preheat the oven to 350°.

Meanwhile, place ingredients for brown sugar crumble in food processor with steel blade. Pulse just until combined. Spread evenly over the top of the toast. Bake for 45 minutes until puffy and golden. Cover with foil for the last five to ten minutes of baking so it doesn't get too dried out. This can be made in advance and stored in the freezer until needed. Serves eight.

BASIC QUICHE

- 1 (9-inch) pie shell
- 1 cup shredded cheese - we use Swiss or Gruyere
- 1 cup chopped, cooked, drained meat or vegetable (we use shrimp, chicken, or broccoli)
- 6 eggs, beaten
- 1-1/2 cups half-and-half, light cream, or milk
- 1/2 teaspoon herb – use your favorite to go with the meat or vegetable of your choice
- 1/2 teaspoon salt

Brush inside of pie shell with a small amount of beaten eggs. Prick the bottom and sides with a fork and bake shell in preheated 450° oven for five minutes. If using a metal pie pan, bake at 425° until golden brown. Set shell aside. Reduce heat to 350°. Put cheese and meat or vegetable in pie shell. Add remaining ingredients to beaten eggs. Beat until well blended. Pour over cheese mixture. Bake 30 to 35 minutes or until knife inserted near center comes out clean. Let stand 5 minutes before serving.

BREAKFAST CROCKPOT CASSEROLE – *Cooks while you sleep!*

- 1 (30 ounce) bag frozen hash browns
- 12 eggs
- 1 cup milk
- 1 tablespoon ground mustard
- 1 teaspoon salt
- 1 teaspoon freshly ground pepper
- 1 (16 ounce) roll of sausage, any flavor
- 16 ounces shredded cheddar cheese

Spray crock pot. Evenly spread hash browns on the bottom of the pot. Crack eggs in a large bowl and whisk until blended. Add milk, ground mustard, salt, and pepper. Mix well and set aside. Cook the sausage on high heat, drain, and put in crock pot on top of the potatoes. Add the cheddar cheese to the pot and mix it all together. Pour the egg mixture over everything and spread it out evenly. Turn the crockpot on low and cook for 6 to 8 hours.
All you have to do in the morning is make coffee!

Nothing to do on a rainy afternoon? Make these muffins and freeze them for another day. They are great to have "on hand" not only for breakfast, but for late night snacks as well.

BREAKFAST MUFFINS

1 cup light mayonnaise
10 slices crumbled bacon or sausage
12 hard-boiled eggs, chopped finely
1/2 teaspoon celery salt
12 ounces shredded cheddar cheese
8 ounces cream cheese, room temperature (light may be used)
1 package English Muffins

Preheat oven to 400°. Mix all ingredients, except muffins, together. Spread 1/4-inch thick on muffins. Bake 15-20 minutes. (15 minutes for softer muffins, 20 minutes for crispy muffins)

<u>To freeze ahead:</u> Bake muffins. Then place two muffins separated on aluminum foil, fold foil over two muffins. Repeat until all are wrapped. Freeze. <u>To serve:</u> Thaw muffins and reheat in 400° preheated oven for approximately ten minutes.

BRUNCH ENCHILADAS

- 2 cups ground ham, fully cooked
- 1/2 cup sliced green onions
- 1/2 cup chopped green pepper
- 2-1/2 cups shredded cheddar cheese
- 8 (7-inch) flour tortillas
- 4 eggs, beaten
- 2 cups milk
- 1 tablespoon flour
- 1/4 teaspoon salt
- 1/4 teaspoon ground pepper
- Few drops bottled hot pepper sauce

In bowl, combine ham, onion, and green pepper. Place 1/2 cup of mixture and three teaspoons shredded cheese on each tortilla. Roll up and place on greased 12x7 baking dish. Combine rest of ingredients. Pour over top of tortillas. Cover and refrigerate for several hours. Bake at 350° for 45-50 minutes. Sprinkle with remaining cheese. Bake three minutes or until cheese melts. Let stand for ten minutes. We suggest serving the following accompaniments on the side: salsa, sour cream, sliced black olives, and more green onions.

BRUNCH FRUIT CUP

- 1 (3 ounce) package lemon Jell-O
- 2 cups boiling water
- 1 (6 ounce) can frozen orange juice
- 1 (20 ounce) can pineapple chunks, undrained
- 1 (11 ounce) can mandarin oranges, undrained
- 1 banana

Dissolve Jell-O with water. Stir in the orange juice until well blended. Add pineapple and oranges. refrigerate overnight. Slice the banana into the mixture just before serving.

Light and cool, this is a perfect side dish to include with any breakfast or brunch menu.

CHRIS'S EASY CHEESE SOUFFLE

1 tablespoon butter
6 eggs
1/2 cup cream
1/4 cup grated Parmesan cheese
1/2 teaspoon mustard
1/2 teaspoon salt
1/4 teaspoon pepper
1/2 pound sharp grated cheddar cheese
11 ounces cream cheese, cut bite size

Place all but last two ingredients in blender. Blend until smooth. Add cheddar cheese and cream cheese while motor is running. Butter soufflé dish and dust with Parmesan cheese, tapping out excess. Pour cheese mixture into dish and bake at 375° for 45 minutes until top is golden brown. **Chris's soufflé is delicious paired with fresh fruit and orange juice.**

We probably make GREEN CHILE BRUNCH BAKE more than any other brunch recipe. Besides being easy to prepare, it's a family favorite and leftovers warm up beautifully!

GREEN CHILE BRUNCH BAKE

10 large eggs
4 cups Monterey Jack cheese, shredded
2 cups small-curd cottage cheese
1/2 cup butter, melted
1/4 cup flour
1 teaspoon baking powder
1/2 teaspoon salt
2 (2-ounce) cans chopped green chilies
Sour cream
Salsa

In a large mixing bowl, beat eggs until well blended. Stir in cheeses, melted butter, flour, baking powder, and salt until well mixed. Stir in chilies. Pour into a sprayed 13x9x2-inch baking dish. Bake in a 350° oven for about 35 minutes or until eggs are set. Cool for ten minutes. Cut into squares and serve with salsa and sour cream. Makes ten servings. May be prepared the night before.

HOT FRUIT – *Thanks Peggy!*

1 (14.5 ounce) can peaches, sliced
1 (14.5 ounce) can pears, sliced
1 (14.5 ounce) can pineapple chunks
1 (21 ounce) can cherry pie filling
8 ounces cinnamon applesauce
1/4 cup brown sugar
1 teaspoon cinnamon

Drain peaches, pears, and pineapple. Mix together and add cherry pie filling and applesauce. Place in baking dish and top with sugar and cinnamon mixture. Bake at 350° for 40 to 45 minutes. **This is a sweet addition to a breakfast or brunch.**

HUEVOS RANCHERO – *Rancher's Eggs*

4 six-inch tortillas
Butter
1 medium onion, diced
1 (12 ounce) can diced tomatoes
Salt
Pepper
Oregano
4 eggs
Optional: sour cream and fresh avocado

Sauté tortillas in butter and set aside. Sauté green pepper and onion in butter until soft. Add tomatoes. Season to taste and simmer for 10 minutes. Make 4 depressions in sauce, and add an egg to each depression. Cook to desired doneness, basting occasionally. Place an egg on each tortilla and spoon sauce over the top. Serve immediately. Mom and I serve sour cream and bite sized pieces of avocado on the side. Makes four servings with one egg each. **Most of our food-loving gang can eat two!**

OVERNIGHT FRENCH TOAST CASSEROLE WITH STRAWBERRIES

1 (1 pound) loaf French bread, cut into 1/2-inch slices
3 ounces nonfat cream cheese, softened
3/4 cup sliced strawberries
3 tablespoons powdered sugar (some extra for topping, optional)
1 cup egg substitute
2 egg whites
1/3 cup skim milk
1/2 teaspoon vanilla extract
Butter-flavored cooking spray
Syrup or preserves (optional)

Spray 9x13-inch baking dish with cooking spray. Arrange half the bread slices in a single layer in dish. Combine cream cheese, 1/2 cup strawberries, and powdered sugar in bowl. Mix until smooth and creamy. Spread 2 tablespoons mixture on each bread slice in baking dish. Top with remaining bread to form sandwiches.

Combine egg substitute, egg whites, milk, and vanilla in a medium bowl; beat mixture until creamy and frothy. Pour mixture over sandwiches. Cover pan with plastic wrap and refrigerate overnight.

After setting overnight, preheat oven to 375°. Line baking sheet with foil and spray with cooking spray. Using slotted spoon, transfer sandwiches to baking sheet; discard remaining egg mixture. Bake 12 to 15 minutes. Turn sandwiches and bake an additional 10 to 15 minutes, until golden brown. Top with remaining strawberry mixture and powdered sugar. Syrup and/or strawberry preserves may be served with casserole. Serves six.

SPINACH, BACON, & MUSHROOM QUICHE

6 large eggs, beaten
1-1/2 cups cream
1/4 teaspoon salt
1/4 teaspoon pepper
1-1/2 cups fresh spinach, chopped
1 cup mushrooms, sliced
1-1/2 cups shredded Swiss cheese
1 (9-inch) pie crust

Prepare crust and place in quiche dish. Combine eggs, cream, salt, and pepper until well blended. Layer the spinach, mushrooms, bacon, and cheese in pie crust. Pour the egg mixture on top. Bake at 375° for approximately 40 minutes until mixture is set.

THEO'S TOAST WITH AVACADO & FRESH TOMATO

Bread, sliced
Butter
1/2 avocado for each slice of toast
1 tablespoon lemon juice per 1/2 avocado
Salt and pepper to taste
Tomato slices
Fresh basil, cleaned and cut into small pieces

Toast and lightly butter the bread. Cut avocado in half, remove pit, and scoop the flesh away from the skin and into a bowl. Sprinkle with lemon juice, salt, and pepper. Lightly mash with fork, leaving it a little chunky. Spread on toast, add slices of fresh tomato and top with fresh basil.

Mom's tip: add melted Brie cheese to the top for an extra touch of yummy!

TOMATO FLORENTINE QUICHE

- 1 (10 ounce) package frozen chopped spinach, thawed
- 1 (14.5 ounce) can petite diced tomatoes, drained
- 2 tablespoons Italian-seasoned bread crumbs
- 2 large eggs, lightly beaten
- 1 cup half-and-half
- 3 bacon slices, cooked and crumbled
- 1/2 cup shredded sharp cheddar cheese
- 1/2 cup shredded mozzarella cheese
- 1 teaspoon pesto seasoning or dried basil
- 1/4 teaspoon ground red pepper
- 1 (9-inch) deep-dish piecrust, unbaked

Drain and squeeze spinach. Set aside. Toss together tomatoes and breadcrumbs. Stir together spinach, eggs, half-and-half, bacon, and next four ingredients in a large bowl. Gently fold in tomato mixture. Place piecrust in deep-dish pie pan. Pour mixture into piecrust and place pan on a baking sheet. Bake at 350° for 50-60 minutes. Remove from oven and let stand 20 minutes before cutting. Garnish with parsley for a perfect presentation.

VIVIAN'S COTTAGE CHEESE PANCAKES

- 4 eggs (or 1 carton egg beaters)
- 3/4 cup flour, whole wheat or white
- 3/4 teaspoon baking powder
- 3/4 teaspoon baking soda
- 1/4 cup powdered milk
- 1 cup cottage cheese, low-fat
- 1/2 cup non-fat yogurt or sour cream
- Serve with butter and maple syrup

Blend all ingredients thoroughly using a hand mixer. Let batter stand ten minutes. Coat medium grill with cooking spray and place over medium-high heat. Place 1/4 cup batter for each pancake onto grill. Flip and cook other side when batter begins to bubble.

The recipe says it feeds four, but we find that they go fast!

SOUPS

Soup is a great meal to have simmering on the stove when you are expecting out-of-town guests. There is no way to know exactly what time the horse-drawn carriage will arrive from the dock or airport, so our sweet Sophie keeps a lookout to announce arrivals.

BEACH-BAR TOMATO SOUP

BEAN & HAM SOUP

BROCCOLI CHEESE SOUP

BROCCOLI, WHITE BEAN, & CHEDDAR SOUP

CREAMY TOMATO SOUP

EASY TURKEY CHILI

GAZPACHO

MAX'S ONION SOUP

OHIO CHILI

ROASTED CAULIFLOWER SOUP

STRAWBERRY SOUP

TURKEY CHILI

VICHYSSOISE

WATERCRESS SOUP

WHITE BEAN CHILI

Don't be fooled by the title. This is not just for beach days! My grandparents used to make this hearty soup on winter days in Michigan. We find it works well on cold Mackinac Island days in spring and fall as well!

BEACH-BAR TOMATO SOUP

2   ounces butter
6   (10-3/4 ounce) cans tomato soup
8   ounces cream cheese, cut in small pieces
2   (14.5 ounce) cans diced stewed tomatoes
1   (8.75 ounce) can evaporated milk
1/2   cup milk
Mozzarella cheese
Garlic croutons

Combine butter, soup, cheese, tomatoes, and milks together. Heat over medium heat stirring constantly until hot. Sprinkle with shredded mozzarella cheese and garlic croutons on top of each serving.

BEAN & HAM SOUP

- 3 (15.8 ounce) cans northern beans, divided
- 1 (14 ounce) can chicken broth, divided
- 2 tablespoons butter
- 1 small onion diced
- 8 ounces cooked ham, cubed
- 1/4 teaspoon pepper

Rinse and drain beans. Process 1/3 beans and half of chicken broth in a food processor until smooth. Melt butter in a Dutch oven over medium heat. Add onion and sauté five minutes or until onion is tender. Add ham and sauté ten minutes or until lightly browned, stirring constantly. Add bean puree, remaining beans, and remaining broth. Bring to a boil; reduce heat, and simmer ten minutes. Stir in pepper. Serve immediately.

BROCCOLI CHEESE SOUP

- 1/2 cup onion, chopped
- 3/4 cup butter
- 3/4 cup flour
- 1 teaspoon pepper
- 1 teaspoon salt
- 3 cups chicken broth
- 4-1/2 cups milk
- 3 cups fresh broccoli, chopped, cooked
- 3/4 cup cheddar cheese, grated

Sauté onion in butter until tender; stir in flour, salt, and pepper. Cook and stir until smooth and bubbly; add broth and milk. Cook and stir until mixture boils and thickens. Reduce heat, add broccoli, and simmer while stirring until soup is heated through. Remove from heat and stir in cheese until melted.

When our daughters were young children, they thought that soup was a great way to eat green vegetables! Actually, they still do!

BROCCOLI, WHITE BEAN, & CHEDDAR SOUP

1 (14 ounce) can reduced-sodium chicken broth
1 cup water
6 cups broccoli crowns, trimmed and chopped
1 (14 ounce) can white beans, rinsed
1/4 teaspoon salt
1/4 teaspoon white pepper
1 cup shredded extra sharp cheddar cheese

Bring broth and water to boil on medium heat. Add broccoli, cover and cook about eight minutes, until tender. Stir in beans, salt, and pepper and continue cooking for one minute, until beans are heated through. Puree in blender little at a time. Blend in cheddar cheese. Serve warm. Makes almost six cups.

CREAMY TOMATO SOUP

1 medium onion, diced
2 tablespoons butter
1 (14 ounce) can tomatoes
2 (10-3/4 ounce) cans tomato soup
1/2 teaspoon paprika
1-1/2 cups milk
1/2 teaspoon basil
1 teaspoon sugar
1/4 teaspoon garlic powder
8 ounces cream cheese, cubed

In large pot, sauté onion in butter. Mix all remaining ingredients, except cheese, and bring to a simmer. Add cream cheese and stir until cheese is melted.

This rich Creamy Tomato Soup is a delicious choice for an appetizer at the beginning of a formal dinner. We also serve it with a good, crusty bread for a hearty family dinner. Either way, everyone sharing your table will be delightfully satisfied.

*Short on time?
Make this quick and easy chili!*

EASY TURKEY CHILI

1 pound ground turkey
1/2 (10 ounce) package frozen chopped onions
2 packages Madras Lentils

Brown turkey, add onions and cook till tender. Add the lentils and heat until hot. Serve in bowls with hard rolls and shredded cheddar cheese.

Gazpacho is a delicious cold soup which comes from Andalusia, a southern region of Spain. It is thought that gazpacho was introduced to Spain by the Romans in ancient times. There are many modern variations, but this one is our favorite. Enjoy!

GAZPACHO

3 large tomatoes, peeled
1 small red or green bell pepper
1 small cucumber
1/2 onion
2 cloves garlic, minced
2 slices white bread

1/2 cup olive oil
1/4 cup white wine vinegar
1-1/4 cups chicken stock
Salt and freshly ground pepper to taste
Garnishes: diced tomato, cucumber, and croutons

Remove seeds from tomatoes, bell pepper, and cucumber. Peel onion. Cut into small pieces. Remove crust from bread and cut into small pieces. Put all ingredients in a bowl and stir. In small batches, puree in a food processor. Put puree in container and refrigerate overnight. Serve cold with garnishes on the side. **Perfect on a hot summer day!**

MAX'S ONION SOUP

4 cups thinly sliced yellow onions
2 tablespoons butter
Pinch of sugar
2 tablespoons flour
2 cups beef bouillon
3 cups water
A generous shot of scotch
1 bay leaf
1/2 teaspoon salt
8 grinds of fresh pepper
6 rounds of stale bread, sautéed in butter
6 slices Gruyere cheese
6 cocottes (small oven-proof bowls)

Sauté onions in the butter and sugar over low heat for 15 to 20 minutes until they are soft and beginning to gently brown. Add the flour and cook for 2 minutes, stirring with a wooden spoon. Bring bouillon, water, and scotch to a boil, stirring all the while. Add the seasonings and simmer, partly covered, over low heat for 25 minutes.

Preheat the broiler. Place the cocottes on a cookie sheet and ladle soup into each one. Quickly place a crouton in each cocotte and top with a slice of cheese, allowing the corners of the cheese to drape over the edge. Broil until the cheese is beginning to brown and is positively bubbly. Serve very hot.

OHIO CHILI

2 pounds ground beef
2 medium onions, chopped
4 garlic cloves, minced
1 tablespoon cocoa
1 tablespoon Worcestershire sauce
4 tablespoons chili powder
1 (15 ounce) jar spaghetti sauce
1-2/3 cups clear beef broth
1 tablespoon ground cumin
1/4 teaspoon cayenne pepper
Salt to taste

In large saucepan over medium heat, cook the beef until light brown. Pour off excess fat. Add remaining ingredients, mix well, and bring to a boil. Stirring as needed, simmer covered until a soupy consistency, about 30 minutes.

ROASTED CAULIFLOWER SOUP

1 head cauliflower, roasted
1 tablespoon olive oil
1/4 teaspoon salt
1/8 teaspoon pepper
1/2 medium onion, sliced
3 cloves garlic, sliced
2 cups reduced-sodium chicken broth
1 tablespoon lemon juice

To roast cauliflower: Heat oven to 400°. Cut cauliflower into florets. Toss with one tablespoon olive oil, 1/4-teaspoon salt, and 1/8-teaspoon pepper. Place on a baking sheet. Roast for 25 minutes, turning once halfway through, until browned.

Soup: Heat remaining olive oil in large pot over medium heat. Sauté onion till softened. Stir in garlic and cook two minutes. Add cauliflower, chicken broth and one cup water. Bring to boil. Cover, reduce heat to a low simmer and cook ten minutes. Transfer soup to blender and process until smooth. Return to pot, stir in lemon juice.

For a special fall treat, cut acorn squash in half and clean out seeds. Place in baking dish and season the cut sides with a little butter, salt, and pepper. Roast in the oven and use as bowls for the Cauliflower Soup. Delicious and very pretty!

SHAREL'S STRAWBERRY SOUP – *cold and refreshing*

2 cups strawberries
1 cup plain yogurt
1 cup milk
3 tablespoons brown sugar
1 teaspoon lemon juice
1 teaspoon vanilla
Strawberry slices for garnish

Place all ingredients in a blender and process until smooth. Serve chilled topped with strawberry slices. Serves four.

Mackinac Island Cottage Cookbook

TURKEY CHILI

2 cups onions, diced
3 cloves garlic, minced
2 tablespoons cooking oil
2 pounds ground turkey
2 (15.8 ounce) cans pinto beans
1 (26 ounce) jar marinara sauce
2/3 cup water
2/3 tablespoons chili powder
1 teaspoon ground cumin
Salt and pepper to taste

Sauté onion and garlic in oil. Add turkey and brown. Add beans, marinara sauce, water, chili powder, cumin, salt, and pepper. Simmer uncovered 1-1/2 hours, stirring frequently.

VICHYSSOISE

1 medium onion, grated
3 cubes chicken bouillon
1 cup water
1/4 teaspoon salt
1/2 cup milk

1-1/4 cups instant mashed potatoes
1-1/2 cups milk
1 cup light cream
Fresh chives, snipped

Combine onion, bouillon cubes, water, and salt in large saucepan. Heat to boiling. Cover and simmer for 10 minutes. Remove from heat. Add 1/2 cup milk. Stir in instant dry potatoes and whip with fork until fluffy. Gradually stir in 1-1/2 cups milk and heat just to boiling. Cover and chill thoroughly. Just before serving, stir in cream and beat until well mixed. Spoon into small bowls and sprinkle with chives.

WATERCRESS SOUP

- 3 medium potatoes
- 3 tablespoons butter
- 2 cups hot milk
- 1-1/4 cups chicken stock
- 1 teaspoon salt
- 1/2 teaspoon pepper
- Small bunch of watercress
- 3 tablespoons light cream

Mom's tip for soup: Use a blender when making cream soups. The key to a successful watercress soup is a really creamy potato puree. This technique works beautifully with other cream soups as well.
Important! Make sure you have the top on tight before you turn on the blender!

Boil potatoes in their skins until tender. Drain, peel, and mash thoroughly. Using a whisk or wooden spoon, stir in butter and 3 to 4 tablespoons of milk, beating until smooth and creamy. Blend in remaining milk and add the chicken stock. Add salt and pepper and bring to a boil. Clean and finely chop watercress. Add to the soup and simmer gently for 3 minutes. Stir in cream and serve immediately. This can also be served chilled, but be sure to stir it occasionally during the cooling process and again just before serving.

WHITE BEAN CHILI – *our compliments to Mil!*

- 1-1/2 chicken breasts, cut in bite size pieces
- 1 tablespoon olive oil
- 1 (48 ounce) jar northern beans
- 1 (16 ounce) jar thick chunky mild salsa
- 2 teaspoons cumin
- 8 ounces Monterey Jack cheese, shredded

Brown chicken in oil about ten minutes. Add everything but cheese. Heat 10-15 minutes stirring occasionally. Just before serving, stir in cheese until melted. Serve with warm crusty bread and butter.

SALADS & DRESSINGS

More salad please! Our visiting friends have shared many tasty salad recipes with our family over the years. Now, our adult kids love salads and make use of those cooking tips learned in our old-fashioned cottage kitchen.

SALADS

BACON, TOMATO, & POTATO SALAD

BROCCOLI SALAD

BROCCOLI & CREAMY FETA SALAD

BUFFET SALAD

CHICKEN SALAD

CHICKEN SALAD FOR SIX OR THIRTY

CORNED BEEF SALAD

CRUNCHY PEA SALAD

CUCUMBERS IN SOUR CREAM

EASY SHRIMP SALAD

FRESH SPINACH SALAD

JELL-O RIBBON SALAD

LAYERED COBB SALAD

LAYERED SPINACH SALAD

MACARONI SALAD

MARCIA'S SALAD

SEVEN-LAYER SALAD

SHRIMP SALAD

SPINACH SALAD WITH BLUE CHEESE

SPINACH TARRAGON SALAD

TACO SALAD

TACO SALAD - JILL'S EASY & TASTY

DRESSINGS

CELERY SEED DRESSING

CHUNKY BLUE CHEESE DRESSING

FRUIT SALAD DRESSING

FRUIT SALAD LIME DRESSING

JANET'S DRESSING

KATIE'S BACON DRESSING

NANCY'S VINAIGRETTE

PEACH FRUIT DRESSING

SOUTHWEST DRESSING

THOUSAND ISLAND DRESSING

BACON, TOMATO & POTATO SALAD

1 pound small red potatoes
1/2 stalk celery, chopped
1/2 medium green bell pepper, julienned
1/4 medium white onion, minced
1/3 cup bacon, fried crispy and crumbled
1 tomato, chopped

Dressing
1/4 cup mayonnaise
1/4 cup sour cream
1-1/2 teaspoons Dijon mustard
1-1/2 teaspoons white vinegar
1/2 teaspoon salt
1/4 teaspoon black pepper

In large saucepan, cook potatoes with skins on. Cool. Cut potatoes into bite-sized pieces. In a large bowl, combine potatoes and remaining salad ingredients, except for tomato. In a small bowl, combine all dressing ingredients. Pour over potato mixture. Toss gently to mix. Add tomato and toss gently. Cover. Refrigerate to chill. Serves six to eight.

"Here Kitty, Kitty, Kitty!"

BROCCOLI SALAD

1 large bunch fresh broccoli flowerets, cut in small pieces
1/4 cup red onion, chopped
1-1/2 ounces real bacon bits
1/2 cup golden raisins
1/2 cup dried sunflower seeds

Dressing:
1 cup mayonnaise
Sugar to taste (about 1/4 cup)
1 tablespoons apple vinegar

This salad will remain fresh for several days which makes it a great make-ahead recipe.

Prepare and combine all salad ingredients. Mix dressing ingredients until smooth. Toss with salad and refrigerate.

BROCCOLI & CREAMY FETA SALAD

1/2 cup crumbled feta cheese
1/2 cup nonfat plain yogurt or sour cream
1 tablespoon mayonnaise
2 tablespoons lemon juice
1 clove garlic, minced
1/4 teaspoon pepper, freshly ground
2-1/2 to 3 cups broccoli crowns, trimmed and finely chopped
1 (7 ounce) can chickpeas, rinsed
1/2 cup chopped red bell pepper

Combine the cheese, sour cream, mayonnaise, lemon juice, garlic, and pepper. Whisk until well blended. Add vegetables and toss to coat. Serve room temperature or chilled.

BUFFET SALAD

1 bunch romaine lettuce, bite size
1 head iceberg lettuce, bite size
1/2 pound fresh mushrooms, sliced
1 large red onion, sliced
1 avocado, diced
2 tomatoes, diced
1/3 cup olive oil
1/4 cup wine vinegar
1/2 cup freshly shredded Parmesan cheese
Garlic salt to taste (about 1 teaspoon)
Pepper to taste

Prepare all vegetables and avocado. Place in a salad bowl. Combine the oil, vinegar, cheese, garlic salt, and pepper. Whisk until well blended. Pour on salad ingredients and toss. Serves ten.

CHICKEN SALAD

Dressing:
1 cup mayonnaise
4 teaspoons apple cider vinegar
5 teaspoons honey
2 teaspoons poppy seeds
Salt and pepper to taste

Salad:
2 pounds boneless skinless chicken breast, cooked
3/4 cup pecan pieces, toasted
2 cups red seedless grapes, sliced in half
3 stalks celery, thinly sliced

Combine all dressing ingredients and refrigerate until ready to use. It may be prepared two days prior to serving. Cut chicken into bit-size chunks and place in a large bowl. Add the pecans, grapes, and celery. Fold in the prepared dressing and serve on a bed of lettuce with additional fruit. Serves six to eight.

CHICKEN SALAD FOR SIX OR THIRTY

4   cups cooked chicken, bite size
1   cup toasted pecans
1   cup celery, chopped
1   small can sliced water chestnuts, halved or quartered

<u>Dressing:</u>   Approximate. (Last 3 ingredients to taste)
1   ounce peach yogurt
1   ounce Hellman's mayonnaise, same amount as yogurt
1/4   teaspoon (rounded) ginger
1/4   teaspoon nutmeg
2   tablespoons (heaping) powdered sugar

Prepare chicken and add remaining ingredients. Combine dressing ingredients and pour over chicken. Mix well. Serves six.

For 30 one-cup servings, increase ingredient amounts as listed below:

20   cups diced chicken (1/2-breasts, 18)
5   cups toasted pecans
5   cups celery, chopped
5   small cans sliced water chestnuts , halved or quartered
5   batches dressing

This has become one of our preferred recipes for special occasion lunches. Add fresh fruit and a croissant to the plate for a beautiful presentation. Always a success!
For easier preparation, we sometimes use already-cooked chicken. It can usually be found in the refrigerated section of most grocery stores.

CORNED BEEF SALAD

1 (3 ounce) package lemon Jell-O
1-1/2 cups hot water
1 cup mayonnaise
1 tablespoon onion flakes
1 cup sour cream
1-1/2 cups celery, diced
3 hardboiled eggs, finely chopped
1 can corned beef, chopped

The best way to describe this recipe is old-fashioned and yummy. It was served at my bridesmaid's luncheon on the day of our wedding in 1974. Of course, I was a little too nervous to eat much, but my sister and friends loved every bite! We'll put this in the Retro column and hope you will give it a try!

Prepare Jell-O with hot water; let cool but do not set. Combine mayonnaise, onion flakes, sour cream, celery, eggs, and corned beef. Fold mixture lightly into Jell-O and pour into a 9X9 pan. Refrigerate until set. Serve on a bed of lettuce. Serves six to nine.

CRUNCHY PEA SALAD

2 (9 ounce) packages frozen peas
2 cups celery, sliced
1 cup coarsely chopped radishes
1/2 cup green onions, sliced
1-1/2 cups sour cream
1 tablespoons vegetable oil
2 tablespoons lemon juice
1/2 teaspoon Dijon mustard
1 teaspoon salt
1/4 teaspoon pepper
Shredded lettuce

Combine peas, celery, radishes, and green onions in a medium-sized bowl. Combine sour cream, oil, lemon juice, mustard, salt, and pepper in a small bowl. Fold into vegetable mixture. Cover with plastic wrap and chill overnight. Serve on shredded lettuce.

Let's hear it for another make-ahead idea! We love recipes that are ready to go, especially after spending an afternoon with our family and friends enjoying Island activities.

We have a friend who loves Cucumbers in Sour Cream. Since he is a regular at our annual Fourth of July gathering, we use this recipe as part of our celebration menu just for him. Well, actually, we really like it too!

CUCUMBERS IN SOUR CREAM

2 cucumbers, sliced thin
1-1/2 teaspoons salt
1 onion, sliced thin
3 tablespoons vinegar
1 cup sour cream
1/4 teaspoon sugar
1/8 teaspoon black pepper

Let cucumbers stand ten minutes with salt. Remove excess liquid. Combine all remaining ingredients and add to cucumbers. Chill at least two hours.

EASY SHRIMP SALAD

1/2 large green cabbage, shredded
1 pound medium cooked shrimp
3/4 cup ranch-style dressing
1 tablespoon fresh lemon juice
1 tablespoon dried dill weed

Shred cabbage, then add all remaining ingredients and toss well. Serves six to eight.

FRESH SPINACH SALAD

Dressing:
1/2 cup mayonnaise
1/4 cup milk
1/4 cup sugar
1/4 cup onion, chopped
1 tablespoon vinegar

Salad:
1 pound fresh baby spinach, washed and dried
4 hard-boiled eggs, chopped
6 slices bacon, extra crisp, bite sized
1 sweet onion, chopped

Mix together all dressing ingredients. Shake well and chill at least 30 minutes. Combine spinach, eggs, bacon, and sweet onion in salad bowl. Add dressing and toss.

JELL-O RIBBON SALAD

1 (6 ounce) box black cherry Jell-O
1 (6 ounce) box peach Jell-O
1 (6 ounce) box red raspberry Jell-O
2 cups sour cream

Easy to make, but time consuming. You have to allow for each layer to set-up before adding the next. Mom's tip: Take the time to make it anyway, because it is always appreciated and the six layers present a beautiful rainbow of color!

Dissolve black cherry Jell-O in 2-1/2-cups boiling water. Pour half into 9x13-inch pan. Let set. Once set, mix 2/3-cup sour cream with remaining half and pour over the first layer. Repeat with the other Jell-O's making sure each step is set before adding the next. Cut in squares. Serve atop a lettuce leaf on a salad plate. Be prepared to share the recipe!

LAYERED COBB SALAD

8 cups chopped iceberg or romaine lettuce
1 cup radishes, thinly sliced
1 cup celery, thinly sliced
3/4 cup onion, finely chopped
2 cups shredded smoked Gouda or extra sharp cheddar cheese
8 hard-cooked eggs, chopped
8 slices thick-cut bacon, cooked and crumbled

Dressing
1 cup light mayonnaise
1 tablespoon sugar
2 tablespoons lemon juice
1/2 teaspoon salt
1/2 teaspoon pepper

Layer lettuce, radishes, celery, onion, cheese, eggs, and bacon in a large salad bowl, or a 9x13-inch pan. Whisk dressing ingredients together in medium bowl. Spoon and gently spread dressing over top of salad. Refrigerate overnight or for at least six hours. Serves ten.

LAYERED SPINACH SALAD – *make it the day before!*

1 pound fresh spinach
Salt, pepper, and sugar, a sprinkle of each
12 slices bacon, crumbled
4 hard-boiled eggs, chopped
1/2 head Romaine lettuce, cut bite size
1 (10 ounce) package frozen tiny peas
1 red onion, chopped
1/2 pound fresh mushrooms, sliced

Dressing
1 teaspoon sugar
2 cups mayonnaise
1 cup sour cream
1 cup Swiss cheese, shredded
Salt and pepper to taste

> Anything that can be made in advance is always a help. It's one less thing to do at dinnertime and gives us more time to be with our guests. To top it off, this salad is yummy.

Layer as listed in large salad bowl or 9x12-inch pan. Blend dressing, spread evenly over the top, and refrigerate for at least 5 hours or overnight. Serves eight to ten.

MACARONI SALAD

2 cups dry elbow macaroni
1/2 cup diced celery
1/2 cup onion, finely chopped
1 tablespoon flat-leaf parsley, minced
1/2 cup vine-ripened tomato, diced
1/2 cup green pepper (optional)
3/4 cup mayonnaise
1 teaspoon dry mustard
1-1/2 teaspoons sugar
1-1/2 tablespoons cider vinegar
1/4 cup sour cream
1/2 teaspoon salt, pepper to taste

Cook, rinse, and drain macaroni. Combine macaroni, celery, onion, parsley, tomato, and green pepper in a large bowl. Whisk together the mayonnaise, mustard, sugar, vinegar, sour cream, salt, and pepper. Pour over the salad and mix well. Chill before serving.

MARCIA'S SALAD

1 can baby lima beans
1/2 can corn kernels
1/2 package peas, frozen
2 tomatoes, chopped
2 cups iceberg lettuce, chopped
1 cup feta cheese
1 bunch green onions, sliced
Buttermilk dressing, purchased

Quite often we have to make do with what is in the pantry, refrigerator, or freezer. Although we have a wonderful grocery store on the Island, it is not always accessible if we are in need of something pronto. The salad is a product of just such a situation. It received great reviews so we continue to make it!

Mix all ingredients together and add dressing to taste or serve on the side. Serves six to eight.

SEVEN-LAYER SALAD

1/2 iceberg lettuce, bite-sized pieces
1/2 cup green onions, sliced
1/2 cup celery, sliced
1 small can water chestnuts, sliced
1 cup carrots, sliced
1/2 cup radishes, sliced thinly
1 cup green pepper, chopped
1 (10 ounce) package frozen tiny peas
Hellman's Real Mayonnaise
1 teaspoon sugar
1/2 cup freshly-grated Parmesan cheese
1/2 pine nuts
Olive oil
2 medium tomatoes, chopped

Place cut lettuce in glass salad bowl. Layer the vegetables in order listed ending with frozen peas. Spread enough mayonnaise on top to cover. Sprinkle sugar over the mayonnaise and then the Parmesan cheese. Cover and refrigerate for 24 hours. Meanwhile sauté pine nuts in olive oil until brown. Cool. Top salad with tomatoes and pine nuts just before serving.

This is not a strict list of vegetables. Use your imagination and add your favorites. We frequently top the salad with chopped hardboiled eggs and crisp, crumbled bacon!

SHRIMP SALAD

Assorted Greens
Shrimp
Corn, frozen
Watermelon
Fresh Mozzarella
Fresh Basil

There are no amounts listed for the ingredients as we prepare this recipe according to the number of people we are serving. It is prepared on individual salad plates.

<u>To prepare:</u>
Cover the salad plate with assorted greens and then add a few medium shrimp. Next scatter 1 to 2 teaspoons of corn and several bite-size watermelon chunks over the greens. Add bites of mozzarella and basil and top with a light dressing. We favor Janet's Dressing (recipe found on page 82) drizzled over the top.

SPINACH SALAD WITH BLUE CHEESE

5 slices bacon, cooked, drained, and crumbled
1/4 cup white wine vinegar
1 teaspoon sugar
1 teaspoon Dijon mustard
1/3 teaspoon salt and pepper
2 tablespoons extra-virgin olive oil
1 pound fresh baby spinach
2 cups seedless red grapes, halved
4 ounces blue cheese, crumbled
Croutons for topping

Cook bacon until crisp, remove to paper towel and reserve drippings. Whisk vinegar, sugar, mustard, salt, and pepper into drippings. Slowly whisk in olive oil until well blended. Place spinach in large bowl and pour warm dressing on top. Add grapes, blue cheese, and bacon pieces. Toss to mix. Top with croutons and serve immediately.

SPINACH TARRAGON SALAD – *Thanks Sharon!*

2 hard boiled eggs, yolks smashed and whites finely chopped
2 tablespoons tarragon vinegar
1 tablespoon Dijon mustard
3 tablespoons shallots, minced
2 tablespoons fresh tarragon leaves, chopped
6 tablespoons olive oil
1/2 pound spinach
10 ounces fresh mushrooms, sliced thin

We have also made this with a mixture of lettuces and topped it with grilled shrimp. It makes a fabulous light dinner.

Whisk yolks, vinegar, and mustard. Add oil and continue to mix until emulsified. Stir in shallots, tarragon, salt, and pepper. Combine spinach, mushrooms, and egg whites. Toss with the dressing and serve. Serve four to six.

TACO SALAD

1 pound ground round
1 large onion, chopped
1 envelope taco mix
3/4 cup water
2 cups iceberg lettuce, chopped
1 can Texas-style beans (heated)
2 tomatoes, chopped
1 bunch green onions, chopped
1 cup black olives, sliced
1 cup salsa, mild
8 ounces shredded cheddar cheese
Sour cream
Guacamole sauce
Tortilla chips or Doritos
Salad Dressing - Thousand Island (recipe on page 84)

Consider serving this salad buffet style, placing each item in an individual bowl. Everyone in our family enjoys designing their own personalized dinner salad.

Guaranteed! No leftovers!

Mom's tip: It's worth it to make the homemade Thousand Island dressing for truly great flavor!

Brown meat and onion; pour off fat. Add taco mix and water and simmer until cooked through, about 5 minutes. Layer the lettuce, beans, tomatoes, green onions, black olives, salsa, and cheese. Top with meat mixture. Serve with sour cream, guacamole sauce, tortilla chips, and homemade Thousand Island dressing.

TACO SALAD – JILL'S EASY & TASTY

Layer the following ingredients in order and serve immediately:

Crushed Doritos
Hot cooked ground beef
Shredded lettuce
Tomatoes
Kidney beans
Shredded cheddar cheese
Thousand Island dressing

CELERY SEED DRESSING

1/2 cup sugar
1 teaspoon celery seed
1/2 teaspoon salt
1/2 teaspoon mustard
1/2 cup cider vinegar
1/2 cup mayonnaise
1 cup vegetable oil

Celery Seed Dressing is an excellent choice for pouring over salad greens. It is also very good over baby spinach with thinly sliced red onions and mandarin oranges. Toss and enjoy!

Place first 6 ingredients in a container. Drizzle vegetable oil slowly into all ingredients and whisk until completely blended. Refrigerate until ready to use.

CHUNKY BLUE CHEESE DRESSING

1 cup mayonnaise
1 cup crumbled blue cheese
4 tablespoons milk
2 tablespoons white vinegar
2 teaspoons sugar
1/4 teaspoon onion powder
1/4 teaspoon dry mustard
1/8 teaspoon garlic powder

Blend all ingredients together. Cover and chill for at least two hours.

FRUIT SALAD DRESSING

1 tablespoon butter
1/2 cup sugar
2 eggs, well beaten
2 lemons, juice only
8 ounces whipping cream

Whisk butter, sugar, eggs, and lemon juice over medium heat until thick. Cool completely. Whip cream until stiff and then fold into the other mixture. Add fresh seasonal fruit.

FRUIT SALAD LIME DRESSING

1/2 cup honey
1 (6 ounce) can frozen limeade concentrate, thawed
1 teaspoon poppy seeds

Whisk together honey, limeade, and poppy seeds in large bowl. Add fruit and toss to coat. Cover. Chill until ready to serve.

JANET'S DRESSING

- 1/2 cup salad oil (not olive oil)
- 1/4 cup red wine vinegar
- 1/4 cup plus 1 tablespoon sugar
- 1/4 teaspoon garlic powder
- 1/4 teaspoon onion powder
- 1/4 teaspoon salt
- 1/4 teaspoon pepper
- 1/4 teaspoon dry mustard

Mix all ingredients together until well blended. Chill and dress your favorite selection of fresh, crisp greens. This will keep well in the refrigerator for several days.

Mom highly recommends serving this dressing at the height of the strawberry season in Michigan. Combine 1-pound fresh spinach, 1-tablespoon fresh chopped dill, 1-teaspoon toasted sesame seeds, and 1-pint fresh strawberries. Pour Janet's dressing over the top, toss gently, and serve! So good!

KATIE'S BACON DRESSING – *Scrumptious on a fresh spinach salad!*

5 slices bacon
2 tablespoons bacon fat
Vegetable oil
3 tablespoons tarragon vinegar
1 teaspoon sugar
1/2 teaspoon dry mustard
1/8 teaspoon salt
1/8 teaspoon pepper

Cut bacon in 1-inch pieces and cook until crisp. Reserve 2-tablespoons of fat. Drain bacon on paper towel. Combine bacon fat with enough vegetable oil to make 1/3-cup. Blend with vinegar, sugar, dry mustard, salt, and pepper. Add cooked bacon to the dressing just before tossing with fresh greens.

NANCY'S VINAIGRETTE

1/2 cup extra virgin olive oil
1/4 cup red wine vinegar
2 cloves minced garlic
1 teaspoon dried oregano
3/4 teaspoon Dijon mustard

Mix all ingredients together with a whisk. Pour into ball jar and shake vigorously. Place in refrigerator for up to four weeks. Perfect for dressing any mixture of fresh greens.

PEACH FRUIT DRESSING

So easy! Just keep a can of peach pie filling on hand at all times. Use it as a dressing for a mixed fruit salad. Quick, easy, delicious, and very refreshing on a hot Mackinac summer day.

SOUTHWEST DRESSING

- 2 cups mayonnaise
- 1 avocado, mashed
- 8 green onions, chopped
- 4 tablespoons buttermilk
- 1 teaspoon hot pepper sauce
- 1/2 teaspoon dry mustard
- 1/4 teaspoon pepper
- 1-1/2 tablespoons Worcestershire sauce
- 1-1/2 tablespoons soy sauce
- 2 teaspoons wine vinegar
- 1 tablespoon fresh lemon juice
- 1/4 teaspoon celery seed
- 1/4 teaspoon oregano
- 1 clove garlic, crushed

Thoroughly mix all ingredients and chill well before serving. Makes 4 cups.

> Both the Southwest dressing and the Thousand Island dressing are perfect selections for a Taco Salad menu. They are equally popular with our gang.

THOUSAND ISLAND DRESSING

- 1 cup mayonnaise
- 1/4 cup chili sauce
- 2 hard boiled eggs, chopped
- 2 tablespoons green pepper, chopped
- 2 tablespoons celery, chopped
- 2 tablespoons onion, chopped
- 1 teaspoon paprika
- 1 teaspoon salt

Mix all ingredients together and chill before serving.

BEEF & PORK

Cooking home-style meals is great fun, but the most enjoyable activity by far is sharing the results with family and friends around the dinner table.

BASIC BRISKET
COCA-COLA RIBS
COUNTRY-STYLE POT ROAST
CRAZY BEEF STEW
CUBED STEAK PARMIGIANINO
EASY BEEF BURGUNDY
ELLEN'S EYE OF ROUND
FAY'S BOURBON PORK TENDERLOIN
FIVE-LAYER CASSEROLE
FLANK STEAK
GARLIC ROAST PORK WITH SUN-DRIED TOMATOES
JILL'S CHILES RELLENOS
MIL'S MEATLOAF – POT ROAST STYLE
MY FAVORITE BEEF STEW
OVEN BEEF BURGUNDY
OVERNIGHT POT ROAST
PEGGY'S SHREDDED BEEF
PORK PATTIES WITH MANDARIN SAUCE
PORK ROAST
PORK STIR FRY WITH PEACHES
PORK TENDERLOIN WITH MAPLE MUSTARD SAUCE
POT ROAST
PULLED PORK
SLOPPY JOES
SLOW COOKED BRISKET
STEAK WITH BLUE CHEESE SPREAD
WHOLE BEEF TENDERLOIN - OVEN ROASTED
MARINADES

BASIC BRISKET

6 pounds brisket of beef
Garlic powder
Salt, pepper
Kitchen Bouquet
1 envelope dried onion soup mix
1 large onion, chopped
1 cup dry red wine

Trim excess fat from brisket and sprinkle lightly with garlic powder, salt, and pepper. Rub lightly with Kitchen Bouquet so that it is brown all over. Place brisket on a double thickness of heavy-duty foil large enough to enclose meat on a cookie sheet or larger roasting pan. Sprinkle onion soup and chopped onion over top of brisket. Adjust foil and pour wine around sides of meat. Seal foil. Bake at 350° for about three hours or until fork tender. Brisket is even better when made ahead and reheated. Pour gravy into a measuring cup, refrigerate and when cold, remove excess fat. Slice meat across grain when cold and reheat in the gravy.

COCA-COLA RIBS

1 slab ribs
2 onions, halved
1 cup Coca-Cola
1 cup barbeque sauce

Parboil ribs with onions. Mix together Coca-Cola and barbeque sauce then pour over ribs. Bake uncovered, basting and turning until tender, about one hour at 350°. Remove from oven and grill just until crispy. Serve with coleslaw and a pile of napkins!

COUNTRY-STYLE POT ROAST

3   plus pounds boneless rump, chuck, or eye of round
1   envelope onion soup mix
2-1/2   cups water
4   medium potatoes cut into 1-inch pieces
4   carrots, sliced
2-4   tablespoons flour

Brown meat over medium high heat. Add soup mix blended with two cups water. Bring to a boil over high heat. Reduce heat to low and simmer covered for two hours, turning roast occasionally. Add vegetables and cook an additional 30 minutes or until veggies and roast are tender. Remove meat & veggies. For gravy, blend remaining 1/2-cup water with flour; stir into drippings, stirring constantly, until thickened. Serves six to eight.

CRAZY BEEF STEW

3   pounds top round
2   onions
3   stalks celery
6   medium carrots
4-5   potatoes
2   teaspoons salt

3   tablespoons tapioca
1   tablespoon sugar
1   bay leaf
2   tablespoon Worcestershire Sauce
1   cup V-8 juice.

Prepare beef and vegetables by cutting in bite-size pieces. Layer in a 3-quart casserole. Mix salt, tapioca, and sugar together and sprinkle over the top. Add a bay leaf. Mix Worcestershire Sauce and V-8 juice together and pour over the casserole. Cover tightly with foil or casserole lid. Bake at 250° for five hours. Do not peek. Serves eight.

Its name is crazy, but the results are insanely good!

CUBED STEAK PARMIGIANINO

6 beef cubed steaks
3 tablespoons flour
1/2 teaspoon salt
1/8 teaspoon pepper
1 egg
2 tablespoons water
1/3 cup fine dry bread crumbs
1/3 cup grated Parmesan cheese
1/4 cup grated Parmesan cheese
1/2 teaspoon basil
3 tablespoons oil
1 (15-ounce) can tomato sauce
1 tablespoon sugar
1 clove garlic, crushed
1/2 plus teaspoon oregano
3 slices (4 ounces) mozzarella cheese, halved

Mix flour, salt, and pepper and place in a flat bowl. Beat egg with 2-tablespoons water and place in flat bowl. Combine bread crumbs, 1/3-cup cheese, and basil and place in flat bowl. Dredge each steak in flour, then in egg mixture, and finally, in crumb mixture, coating evenly.

Put oil in 13x9-inch roasting pan; put in oven and preheat to 375°. Then place breaded steaks in hot pan, return to oven, and bake uncovered for 30 minutes or until golden brown. Pour off the drippings.

Combine tomato sauce, sugar, garlic, and oregano. Pour over meat. Sprinkle with 1/4-cup Parmesan cheese. Bake 20 minutes. Put a halved-cheese slice on each steak and sprinkle a little oregano on top. Bake 3 to 5 minutes or until cheese is melted. Serves six.

EASY BEEF BURGUNDY

1-1/2 pounds stew meat, bite-size, browned
1 (10-3/4 ounce) can cream of mushroom soup
1 envelope onion soup mix
1-1/2 cups burgundy
1 small package egg noodles
Parsley
Butter

Mix first four ingredients together and bake covered for three hours at 300°. Cook noodles al dente, drain, and fold in parsley and butter to taste. Serve the beef Burgundy with noodles. Four servings.

ELLEN'S EYE OF ROUND

4 to 6 pounds eye of round roast
2 tablespoons shortening
1/2 cup dry red wine or Burgundy
1-1/2 cups beef broth
1/2 cup chopped onion
1 teaspoon salt
1/4 teaspoon black pepper
1/4 teaspoon ground thyme
1 bay leaf
1 clove garlic, minced
1/4 cup all-purpose flour

In Dutch oven, brown meat slowly on all sides in hot shortening. Add the red wine, 1 cup of the beef broth, onion, salt, pepper, thyme, bay leaf, and garlic. Cover and roast at 325° for 2-1/2 to 3 hours. Remove roast from pan and transfer to serving platter. Keep warm. Discard the bay leaf.

For gravy, skim off excess fat from pan juices. Add water to juices to make 2 cups. Return juices to pan. Blend remaining 1/2-cup of wine with the flour and add to pan juices. Cook and stir until thickened and bubbly. Serves eight.

FAY'S BOURBON PORK TENDERLOIN

1/2 cup bourbon
1/2 cup dark brown sugar
1/3 cup soy sauce
1/2 bunch fresh cilantro or flat leaf parsley, chopped
1/4 cup lemon juice
2 teaspoons Worcestershire sauce
1 cup water
1/2 teaspoon dried thyme
2 pounds pork tenderloin

Mix all ingredients, except pork, together until brown sugar dissolves. Pour over the pork, cover, and refrigerate for 8 to 12 hours. Turn meat occasionally to evenly marinate. Place tenderloin in a well-greased pan. Roast for 30 minutes at 450° basting frequently with the marinade. Meat thermometer must register at least 145° up to 160°.

FIVE-LAYER CASSEROLE

1-1/2 pounds ground beef
5 pounds potatoes, bite size pieces or sliced
1 large onion, chopped
2 cups chopped celery
1 (10-3/4 ounce) can tomato soup
1/2 cup hot water
Salt and pepper to taste

Place one half of the meat, potatoes, onions, and celery in a one-quart casserole. Pour one half can of soup over the above. Repeat layers and top with hot water and seasonings. Cover and bake for two hours at 300° or until casserole is well done. Serves six.

FLANK STEAK

1-1/2 pounds flank steak
1/4 cup soy sauce
1 tablespoon lemon juice
3 shakes Tabasco
1/2 teaspoon Worcestershire sauce
1/2 teaspoon onion powder
1/2 teaspoon garlic powder

Flank steak has long been part of the grilling fun at the cottage. It is perfect to serve for a casual dinner and our family always requests it. Don't worry about leftovers as they seem to fly right out of the refrigerator! Thank you, Jano Dunnigan, this one is a "keeper"!

Tenderize steak on both sides using a fork. Combine remaining ingredients for marinade and pour over steak. Marinate for at least two hours; however, we think it is best to marinate all day. Grill for 10 to 15 minutes on each side. Cut slices about 1/8 to 1/4-inch thick, angled against the grain. **We serve this with sweet or russet baked potatoes, coleslaw, and corn on the cob.**

GARLIC ROAST PORK WITH SUN-DRIED TOMATOES

- 3 pounds boneless pork loin
- 2 tablespoons extra virgin olive oil, divided
- 4 large garlic cloves, minced
- 1 tablespoon chopped fresh or 2 teaspoons dried rosemary
- 1 teaspoon kosher (coarse) salt
- 1 teaspoon freshly ground pepper
- 1/4 cup dry vermouth or reduced sodium chicken broth
- 1 tablespoon chopped sun-dried tomatoes (not oil packed)

Heat oven to 425°. With sharp knife, make 1-inch slits all around pork. Brush pork with 1-tablespoon oil. In small bowl, stir together garlic, rosemary, and the remaining 1-tablespoon oil. Rub over pork, pushing into slits. Sprinkle with salt and pepper. Place pork on a rack in shallow roasting pan and bake for 30 minutes. Reduce oven temp to 375° and bake an additional 50 to 60 minutes or until internal temperature reaches 145°. Place on cutting board, cover loosely with foil, and let stand for ten minutes. Meanwhile, place roasting pan with drippings over medium heat. Add vermouth and sun-dried tomatoes. Bring to a boil, stirring to scrape up any browned bits from bottom of pan. Boil four to six minutes or until reduced to about one-half cup. Thinly slice pork and top with sauce. Serves eight.

JILL'S CHILES RELLENOS

12 cubanelle peppers
1-1/2 pounds ground beef
1 large onion, chopped
4 cups Monterey Jack cheese, shredded
8 eggs, separated
1 stick butter, melted
2-1/2 tablespoons flour
1/2 teaspoon paprika
1/4 teaspoon cayenne pepper

Steam peppers, cut in half, and remove seeds. Fry ground beef and onions together. Drain. In baking dish, layer half of the peppers and cheese. Add the ground beef mixture and then the remaining peppers and cheese. Separate 8 eggs. Beat egg yolks, melted butter, flour, and seasonings until well blended. Beat egg whites until stiff. Fold stiff egg whites into egg yolk mixture and pour over top of casserole. Bake at 350° for 45 minutes.

MIL'S MEAT LOAF - POT ROAST STYLE

2 pounds ground chuck
2/3 cup evaporated milk
1/3 cup bread crumbs
1/4 teaspoon pepper
1/2 teaspoon salt
1/4 cup catsup
2 teaspoons Worcestershire sauce
4 medium potatoes, sliced 1/4" thick
3 onions, cut in half
1 cup baby cut carrots
2 teaspoons parsley
1 teaspoon salt
Dash pepper
1/4 cup water

Preheat oven to 325°. Make meat loaf by mixing the chuck, milk, bread crumbs, pepper, salt, catsup, and Worcestershire sauce together. Form in a rectangle and place in the middle of a 9x13 pan. Place the vegetables around edge of meat loaf. Mix parsley, salt, and pepper together and sprinkle on the vegetables. Add the water and cover tightly with foil. Bake for two hours. Uncover and bake another thirty minutes to brown. Serves eight.

MY FAVORITE BEEF STEW

4 pounds. chuck roast, cubed
1 (14.5 ounce) can diced tomatoes
1 cup diced celery
6 medium carrots, diced
3 medium onions, sliced
4 large potatoes, cubed

1 can water chestnuts, drained and sliced
1 pound mushrooms, sliced
1 tablespoon sugar
5 tablespoons quick-cooking tapioca
1/4 cup red wine
Salt and pepper to taste

Combine all ingredients in large heavy pan and mix thoroughly. Cover and bake in a 250° oven for six hours. Stir occasionally. Uncover last half hour to brown. Stew will be thick, browned and delicious. Serves eight to ten.

OVEN BEEF BURGUNDY

- 4 slices bacon
- 2 pounds beef round, cut into cubes
- 1/4 cup all purpose flour
- 1/2 teaspoon salt
- 1/4 teaspoon pepper
- 2 tablespoons brandy (optional)
- 12-16 small pearl onions, peeled
- 1/2 pound small fresh mushrooms
- 2 tablespoons chopped fresh parsley
- 3/4 cup condensed beef broth
- 3/4 cup dry red wine
- 2 tablespoons Dijon mustard
- 1/4 teaspoon ground thyme
- 1 small clove garlic, crushed
- 1 bay leaf

Cook bacon until crisp in large skillet, reserving drippings. Remove bacon and crumble. Shake beef with flour, salt, and pepper in plastic bag to coat well. Brown beef in skillet, about half at a time, in hot drippings. Transfer to three-quart casserole. Warm brandy in small saucepan; ignite, then pour flaming brandy over beef. Add onions, mushrooms, and parsley.

Stir broth, wine, mustard, thyme, garlic, and and any remaining flour into drippings in skillet. Heat to boiling, stirring to loosen brown bits. Pour over beef and vegetables. Add bay leaf. Bake, covered for 1-1/2 to 2 hours at 350°, or until tender. Add crumbled bacon and stir. Serves six to ten.

OVERNIGHT POT ROAST

- 1 large onion, sliced
- 3 pounds flank steak
- 2 teaspoons steak seasoning
- 1 envelope onion soup mix
- 1 (14.5 ounce) can stewed Italian tomatoes, undrained
- 3 stalks celery, cut into 1-inch pieces
- 1 (10-3/4 ounce) can condensed cream of celery soup.

Place onion in the bottom of a five-quart slow cooker. Coat flank steak with seasoning; place on top of onion. Sprinkle soup mix over roast and add tomatoes. Cover and cook on low heat setting for eight hours (overnight). In the morning, stir together the celery and celery soup. Spoon into slow cooker. Cover and continue cooking for eight hours more.

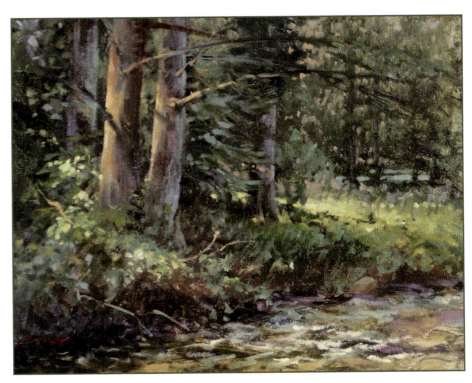

PEGGY'S SHREDDED BEEF

3 pounds rump roast
1 envelope French onion soup
1 quart jar dill pickles with juice
12 sandwich rolls

Cook in slow cooker on medium heat for six to eight hours. Drain juice, remove pickles, shred meat, and serve on rolls. Makes about twelve sandwiches.

PORK PATTIES WITH MANDARIN SAUCE

2 pounds ground pork
Salt and pepper to taste
1 (8-ounce) can water chestnuts
1 (13-1/4 ounce) can pineapple tidbits in heavy syrup
1/3 cup sugar
3 tablespoons cornstarch
1/3 cup vinegar
3 tablespoons soy sauce
1 small green pepper, cut in strips
1/8 teaspoon salt

Shape meat into eight patties about 3/4-inch thick. Put patties on rack in shallow roasting pan. Bake 400° for 30-35 minutes. Season patties with salt and pepper. Serve with mandarin sauce.

Mandarin Sauce:
Drain and cut water chestnuts into six pieces each. Drain pineapple tidbits, reserving syrup. Add water to syrup to make one cup. In saucepan, mix sugar and cornstarch. Gradually add vinegar, soy sauce, and reserved syrup. Heat to boiling; lower heat and cook, stirring constantly, until thickened and clear. Parboil green pepper strips in 1/3 cup salted water for two minutes, stirring occasionally. Drain pepper. Add pineapple and water chestnuts to sauce; heat and add green pepper. Serves eight.

PORK ROAST

2 pounds pork roast
1/2 cup apple vinegar
1/2 cup maple syrup
1 teaspoon Worcestershire sauce
Black pepper
1 tablespoon Dijon mustard

Preheat oven to 350°. Place roast in prepared roasting pan. Mix vinegar, syrup, Worcestershire sauce, pepper, and mustard together and heat. Pour mix over roast and baste often until meat reaches an internal temperature of 145° to 160°. Let roast rest for three minutes before carving.

PORK STIR FRY WITH PEACHES

2 boneless butterfly pork chops (about 1/2 pound)
1/4 teaspoon salt
1/2 teaspoon white pepper
Vegetable cooking spray
1 teaspoon ginger root, peeled, minced
1 tablespoon cornstarch
1/3 cup low-sugar apricot spread
1/4 cup peach nectar
3 cups fresh peaches, sliced
6 ounces snow peas, fresh, trimmed

Trim fat from chops. Partially freeze chops (makes slicing easier) and then slice diagonally across grain into thin strips. Sprinkle with salt and pepper. Set aside. Coat a skillet or wok with cooking spray and place over medium-high heat until hot. Add ginger root; stir-fry 30 seconds. Add sliced chops and stir-fry for three minutes. Blend corn starch with the apricot spread and peach nectar. Add apricot mixture and cook one minute, or until mixture is thickened. Add peaches and snow peas, tossing gently. Cover and cook one minute or until thoroughly heated. Serves six.

PORK TENDERLOIN WITH MAPLE MUSTARD SAUCE

2 pounds pork tenderloin
Salt and pepper
Olive oil
1/2 cup maple sugar
1 teaspoon Worcestershire sauce
1/4 cup cider vinegar
1/2 teaspoon pepper
1 tablespoon Dijon mustard

Season meat with salt and pepper to taste. Brown all sides in oil and place in roasting pan. Mix remaining ingredients together and boil for five minutes in the oil. Brush sauce on meat. Roast for 20 minutes at 375° or until internal temperature reaches 160°. Serves six.

POT ROAST

2 pounds blade-cut chuck roast
2 teaspoons kosher salt
2 teaspoons cumin
Vegetable oil
1 medium onion, chopped
5 cloves garlic, smashed
1 cup tomato juice
1/3 cup balsamic vinegar
1 cup cocktail olives, drained and chopped
1/2 cup dark raisins

Preheat oven to 200°. Rub both sides of meat with the salt and cumin. Place heavy skillet over high heat for two minutes. Brown meat on both sides when pan is really hot. Remove from pan. Add just enough vegetable oil to cover the bottom of the pan, then add the onion and garlic. Stir constantly till onion is softened. Add tomato juice, vinegar, olives, and raisins. Bring to boil and boil slowly until the liquid is reduced by half. Make a pouch with heavy-duty aluminum. Place half the liquid mix on foil, add roast and remaining mixture. Close pouch and wrap tightly in another layer of foil. Cook for 3 to 3-1/2 hours. Remove and let rest for 1/2 hour. Snip corner and drain liquid into a bowl. Add some of the pan drippings to the liquid and puree with a food processor or blender. Slice meat thinly or pull apart with a fork. Serve the sauce on the side. Serves six.

PULLED PORK

3-4 pounds pork butt
1/2 cup brown sugar
6 garlic cloves, chopped
1 sweet onion, chopped
1/2 cup cider vinegar
1 bottle barbeque sauce
Salt and pepper to taste
1-1/2 teaspoons Worcestershire sauce
Sandwich buns

Mix all ingredients except pork and sandwich buns. Place pork in aluminum foil and place in baking dish. Pierce with fork and rub mixture all over the pork. Cover tightly and bake at 225° for 9 hours. If desired, foil may be opened the last hour with temperature at 350°. Remove excess fat and cook juices on top of stove with barbeque sauce. Pull pork apart with two forks. Serve on buns with sauce on the side. This serves many and is just as tasty warmed up the next day. It may also be frozen.

SLOPPY JOES

1 pound lean ground beef
1/2 cup green bell pepper, chopped
1/2 cup onion, chopped
1 cup ketchup
1 tablespoon prepared mustard
2 teaspoons instant beef bouillon
1/4 cup water
2 teaspoons sugar

Brown meat with green pepper and onion, drain off fat. Add remaining ingredients and bring to a boil. Reduce heat, cover, and simmer until ready to serve.

SLOW COOKED BRISKET

2 sweet onions, sliced
3 pounds beef brisket, trimmed
1 envelope dry onion soup mix
1-1/2 cups ketchup
1 (12 ounce) can cola

Coat slow cooker with nonstick cooking spray. Place onions in slow cooker. Season brisket with soup mix and place on top of onions. Combine ketchup and cola; pour over brisket. Cover and cook on low for eight hours. Remove to cutting board. Let rest ten minutes then slice against the grain. Serves six to eight.

STEAK WITH BLUE CHEESE SPREAD

3 ounces cream cheese
3/4 cup crumbled blue cheese
1/4 cup heavy whipping cream
2 tablespoons finely chopped walnuts, toasted
2 tablespoons chopped green onions

Whisk cheeses and cream until blended. Add walnuts and onions. May be made two days ahead. Cover and refrigerate. Serve at room temperature with your favorite steak.

WHOLE BEEF TENDERLOIN - OVEN ROASTED

Season meat with a combination of garlic powder, thyme, rosemary, marjoram, coarsely ground pepper, and dried parsley. Do not use salt. In shallow baking pan, place meat tucking small ends under. Let meat stand at room temperature about one hour before baking. Preheat oven to 400°. Bake 20 minutes. Turn oven down to 325° and bake ten minutes per pound for rare meat or 20 minutes per pound for medium. Check with meat thermometer for accuracy. Let stand five minutes before cutting. Serves eight to twelve.

MARINADES - BEEF & PORK

Immerse beef or pork in a marinade of your choice and let it soak for a period of time. The process tenderizes and enhances the flavor of the meat.
However, Dan's favorite way to prepare steaks for grilling does not involve a sauce, just salt and pepper! Allow steak to reach room temperature. Cover all sides of steak with a heavy layer of salt and pepper and let set for approximately an hour. Grill to desired doneness. The flavor is locked in and absolutely delectable.

PORK TENDERLOIN MARINADE

1/2 cup brown sugar
1/3 cup oil
1/4 cup vinegar
3 cloves garlic
3 tablespoons Poupon mustard
3 tablespoons lemon juice

Poke holes in tenderloin; marinate for at least an hour before grilling.

THE ONLY MARINADE YOU'LL EVER NEED

1/4 cup fresh lemon juice
1/2 teaspoon hot pepper flakes
1/2 teaspoon cracked black pepper
1/2 teaspoon coarse salt (kosher or sea)
4 strips of lemon zest
3 cloves garlic, crushed or minced
1/4 cup fresh parsley, coarsely chopped
1/4 cup fresh basil, cilantro, dill, oregano, or a mix of all four, coarsely chopped
1/2 cup extra virgin olive oil.

Combine first four ingredients in a glass, ceramic, or stainless steel bowl and whisk until salt crystals are dissolved. Add all remaining except oil. Whisk in the olive oil until emulsified. Use within one to two hours of making and be sure to stir again before using.

THE PERFECT RUB – *good for beef and pork*

1 cup kosher salt
1 tablespoon onion powder
1 tablespoon black pepper
3 tablespoons paprika
1 tablespoon dried thyme
1 tablespoon dried mustard
1 teaspoon garlic powder
1 teaspoon hot pepper flakes

Mix all ingredients together. Rub on meat prior to cooking.

CHICKEN

We love the sound of the special chimes at the back door of the cottage. Our daughter Libby brought them from South Korea years ago.

APRICOT-LIME CHICKEN THIGHS

CHICKEN CHEDDAR BAKE

CHICKEN DRESSING BAKE

CHICKEN PATTIES MANDARIN

CHICKEN PICCATA

CHICKEN PIE IN ENGLISH PASTRY

CHICKEN WITH ARTICHOKES/MUSHROOMS

CHICKEN WITH CHEESE

CREAMY CHICKEN ALFREDO

CREAMY CHICKEN ENCHILADAS

CRISPY BAKED CHICKEN

CRUNCHY ONION CHICKEN

EASY BAKED CHICKEN

PANKO ENCRUSTED CHICKEN BREASTS

RITZ CRACKER CHICKEN

SANDY'S HONEY MUSTARD CHICKEN

SIMPLE COCA-COLA CHICKEN

TARRAGON CHICKEN

TRISH'S CHICKEN ROLL-UPS

MARINADES

APRICOT-LIME CHICKEN THIGHS

1/4 cup apricot preserves
2 large garlic cloves, minced
1 tablespoon lime juice
2 teaspoons lime peel, grated
1/2 teaspoon coarse salt
1/3 teaspoon cayenne pepper
8 bone-in chicken thighs, skin removed
1 cup whole-wheat panko
1 teaspoon curry powder
4 lime wedges

Preheat oven to 400°. Line large rimmed baking sheet with foil and coat with cooking spray. Stir all ingredients except chicken, panko, curry powder, and lime wedges in shallow bowl until combined. Stir panko and curry powder in small shallow bowl. Coat chicken with apricot mixture; roll in panko mixture, pressing to coat completely. Place on baking sheet; lightly coat chicken with cooking spray. Bake 30 to 35 minutes until done. Serve with lime wedges. Serves four.

CHICKEN CHEDDAR BAKE

6 chicken breast halves
1/2 cup mayonnaise
1/4 cup shredded cheddar cheese
6 tablespoons bread crumbs

Pound breasts to tenderize. Combine the mayonnaise and shredded cheddar cheese. Roll breasts in mixture, place on prepared baking sheet, and top with the bread crumbs. Bake at 425° for 25 minutes. Serves six.

CHICKEN DRESSING BAKE

8 ounces Pepperidge Farm Stuffing
1 small onion, chopped
4 cups chicken breasts, cubed and cooked
1/2 cup butter
1/2 cup flour

Salt and pepper to taste
4 cups chicken broth
6 eggs, slightly beaten
Paprika

Sauce
1/2 pound fresh mushrooms (canned mushrooms, drained, may be used)
1 tablespoon butter
1 (10-3/4 ounce) cream of mushroom soup
1/4 cup cream
1-1/2 cups sour cream

Prepare stuffing according to directions, add onion and spread in 13x9-inch baking dish. Top with cubed chicken. Melt butter and blend in flour, salt, and pepper until smooth. Add broth and cook, stirring constantly until semi-thick. Mix small amount of hot hot mixture into eggs. Return egg mixture to remaining hot mixture and pour over chicken. Sprinkle with paprika. Bake at 325° for one hour. Let stand five minutes.

Meanwhile, prepare the sauce. Sauté fresh mushrooms in butter until tender. Combine with the remaining sauce ingredients. Heat and serve on the side with the chicken dressing bake.
Serves eight.

CHICKEN PATTIES MANDARIN

2 pounds ground chicken
Salt and pepper
1 (8 ounce) can water chestnuts
1 (13-1/4 ounce) can pineapple tidbits with heavy syrup
1/3 cup sugar
3 tablespoons cornstarch
1/3 cup vinegar
3 tablespoons soy sauce
1 small green pepper, cut in strips
1/8 teaspoon salt

Patties
Shape meat into eight patties about 3/4-inch thick. Put patties on rack in shallow roasting pan. Bake at 400° for 30-35 minutes. Season patties with salt and pepper to taste.

Sauce:
Drain and cut water chestnuts into six pieces each. Drain pineapple, reserving syrup. Add water to syrup to make one cup. In saucepan, mix sugar and cornstarch. Gradually add vinegar, soy sauce, and reserved syrup. Heat to boiling. Lower heat and cook, stirring constantly, until thickened and clear. Parboil green pepper strips in 1/3-cup salted water for two minutes, stirring occasionally. Drain pepper strips. Add pineapple and water chestnuts to sauce. Heat and add green pepper. Serve with the chicken patties. Serves eight.

CHICKEN PICCATA

3 whole chicken breasts
Salt and pepper
1/4 cup flour
2 tablespoons butter
1/2 cup white wine or chicken broth
1 tablespoon lemon juice
Capers, small jar drained
1 lemon, cut into thin slices
Fresh parsley, chopped

Pound meat to 1/4-inch thickness and season. Coat with flour. Cook in skillet with butter until lightly browned (2-3 minutes per side). Remove from skillet and keep warm. Stir wine and lemon juice into pan drippings. Add capers and lemon slices. Cook and stir until thickened. Garnish with fresh parsley. Serves six.

Every visitor to our cottage seems to find something that they love to do. Deadheading flowers is just one of those special activities.

CHICKEN PIE IN ENGLISH PASTRY

1/2 cup celery
1/2 cup onion
1 (10 ounce) package frozen peas
1/8 teaspoon salt
1 tablespoon flour
1 cup water or chicken broth
1/2 cup chopped mushrooms
3 cups cooked chicken, bite size
1 tablespoon lemon juice
3 tablespoons parsley

> *This was my favorite birthday dinner when I was a little girl. I have many fond memories of festive tables with family and friends gathered to enjoy the celebration.*
> *Thanks Mom and Dad!*

Cook celery, onions, and peas in boiling salted water. Mix flour with 1/2-cup stock. Stir until thick and then add to remaining stock. Add mushrooms, chicken, lemon juice, and parsley. Pour into English pastry and bake at 425° for 30 minutes until brown. Serves six.

English Pastry
2 cups flour
2 teaspoons baking powder
1 teaspoon salt
2/3 cup shortening
1/2 cup hot water
1 tablespoon lemon juice
1 egg separated

Sift together the dry ingredients. Mix the shortening, water, lemon juice, and egg yolk together. Stir into flour mixture. Roll out 3/4 for lining and fill with chicken mixture. Top with remaining pastry. Beat egg white and brush over top. Serves six.

CHICKEN WITH ARTICHOKES/MUSHROOMS

1-1/2 teaspoons salt
1/2 teaspoon paprika
1/4 teaspoon pepper
3 pounds chicken breast, pounded
6 tablespoons butter, divided
1/2 pound fresh mushrooms, sliced
2 tablespoons flour
2/3 cup chicken broth
3 tablespoons sherry
1 (14-ounce) can artichoke hearts

Sprinkle the chicken with salt, pepper, and paprika. Brown the chicken in four tablespoons of butter in a frying pan. Place in large casserole. Place two tablespoons of butter in the same frying pan and sauté mushrooms for five minutes. Sprinkle flour over top and stir in chicken broth and sherry. Cook for five minutes. Arrange artichoke hearts between chicken pieces. Pour sauce over them. Cover. Bake at 375° for 40-45 minutes. Serves six.

CHICKEN WITH CHEESE

4 whole boneless chicken breasts
8 slices Monterey Jack cheese
1 (10-3/4 ounce) can cream of chicken soup

1/4 cup dry wine (white)
2 cups seasoned stuffing mix
1/3 cup butter

Cut chicken breast in half, pound, and place in prepared baking dish. Top with slices of cheese. Mix soup and wine and spoon over chicken. Top with stuffing mix. Drizzle butter on top. Bake uncovered at 350° for 50 to 55 minutes. Serves eight.

CREAMY CHICKEN ALFREDO

1/4 cup flour
1/2 teaspoon salt
6 boneless, skinless chicken-breast halves
2 tablespoons plus 1 teaspoon olive oil, divided
3 cloves garlic, minced
1 tablespoon minced onion
1-1/2 cups whipping cream
1/3 cup grated Parmesan cheese
1/2 teaspoon coarsely ground black pepper
1 tablespoon coarsely chopped fresh parsley

We often cook the chicken in advance to minimize preparation time just before dinner. After all, we don't want to miss the cocktail hour and visiting on the porch!

Serve this Creamy Chicken Alfredo with fettuccine, a crisp, leafy green salad lightly dressed, and of course, hot crusty bread.

Preheat oven to 375°. Place flour and salt in a zipper bag. Shake the chicken in flour. Heat 2-tablespoons of olive oil in a large skillet over medium-high heat until hot. Add chicken. Cook, turning once, until golden, 2-4 minutes per side. Remove chicken from skillet and place in a 13x9-inch baking dish. Heat remaining olive oil in the same skillet over medium heat until hot. Add garlic and onion. Cook until garlic is fragrant and onion is tender, 1-2 minutes. Increase heat to medium-high. Add whipping cream, Parmesan cheese, and pepper. Cook until sauce is bubbly and slightly thickened, 2-3 minutes. Spoon sauce over chicken in dish. Bake 8-12 minutes. Sprinkle with parsley and serve over fettuccine. Serves six.

Chicken Enchiladas is one of our tried and true recipes. It is always a success and at the top of our request list for dinner. Although it takes a while to prepare, we have, nevertheless, developed a few short-cuts which save time without affecting the taste and presentation.

Chicken – cook in advance or purchase already cooked and cut-up chicken breast. Skip the step to cook the tortillas. Just use them right out of the package. Not only will it be healthier, but it will not compromise the taste. Promise!

CREAMY CHICKEN ENCHILADAS

4 tablespoons butter
2 small onions, thinly sliced
1-1/2 cups cooked chicken, cut in small cubes
4 tablespoons diced green chilies
6 ounces cream cheese, diced
Salt
Oil
8 flour tortillas
2/3 cup whipping cream
2 cups grated Monterey Jack cheese

Serve with chopped green onions, sliced black olives, lime wedges, sour cream, and salsa.

Preheat oven 375°. Grease 9x13 baking dish. Melt butter in large skillet over very low heat. Add onions and cook until limp, NOT brown. Remove from heat. Add chicken, chilies, and cream cheese. Mix lightly with fork. Add salt to taste.

Heat 1/4-inch oil in small skillet. Dip tortillas, one at a time, and fry several seconds until they begin to blister and become limp, NOT crisp. Remove with tongs and drain on paper towel.

Spoon about 1/3-cup of filling down center of each tortilla. Roll and set seam down in baking dish. Moisten tops with cream. Sprinkle with cheese. Bake uncovered about 20 minutes. Serves four.

CRISPY BAKED CHICKEN

1/4 cup mayonnaise
2 tablespoons Dijon mustard
4 chicken breast halves
2 cups crushed cornflakes
4 tablespoons melted butter

Preheat oven to 375°. Mix mayonnaise and mustard. Drench chicken in mix and roll in cornflakes. Place in prepared baking pan and bake for 50 minutes. Serves four.

CRUNCHY ONION CHICKEN

3 whole chicken breasts, halved and pounded
1 egg, beaten
1-1/2 cups canned French's French-fried onions, crushed

Dip chicken in beaten egg then roll in onion crumbs. Place in baking dish and bake approximately 20 minutes at 400° until cooked through. Serves six.

EASY BAKED CHICKEN

6 chicken breasts halves
1/2 teaspoon garlic salt
1 teaspoon paprika
2 tablespoons fresh parsley
1 (10-3/4 ounce) can cream of mushroom soup
1 cup cream

Place chicken breasts into a prepared pan. Thoroughly mix garlic salt, paprika, and soup. Spoon over chicken and sprinkle with parsley and additional paprika. Bake one hour at 350°.

PANKO ENCRUSTED CHICKEN BREASTS

3/4 cup all-purpose flour
1 teaspoon paprika
Zest of 1 lemon
1/2 teaspoon salt
1/4 teaspoon freshly ground black pepper
1 egg, beaten
1 cup panko
1 pound chicken breast, boneless, skinless, cut crosswise in half
1/2 tablespoon olive oil
2 tablespoons fresh parsley leaves, finely chopped

Preheat oven to 425°. Line a baking sheet with parchment paper. Combine flour, paprika, lemon zest, salt, and pepper in small dish. In a second dish, add the beaten egg. Place panko in a third small dish. Dredge each chicken piece in flour mixture, dip in egg, and then dredge in panko, pressing to coat. Place chicken on a baking sheet and spray with olive oil on both sides. Bake for ten minutes Turn each piece over and continue baking for an additional twelve minutes or until the chicken is cooked through, and golden. Garnish with a lemon slice and chopped parsley.
Serves four.

RITZ CRACKER CHICKEN

3 whole boneless chicken breasts, pounded
1 (10-3/4 ounce) cream of chicken soup
1 cup sour cream
Poppy seeds
1 stack Ritz crackers, smashed
Pats of butter.

Place chicken in baking pan. Mix soup and sour cream together and spread over chicken. Sprinkle with poppy seeds. Sprinkle cracker crumbs over top and add pats of butter. Bake 350° for 50 minutes. Serves six.

SANDY'S HONEY MUSTARD CHICKEN

6 chicken breast halves
1/2 cup honey
1/2 cup mustard
1/4 cup melted butter
1 teaspoon curry

Dip chicken in mixture of honey, mustard, butter, and curry. Place in a prepared pan and bake at 350° for one hour. Serves six.

SIMPLE COCA-COLA CHICKEN

1 cup Coca-Cola
1 cup barbeque sauce
1 chicken cut in pieces

Mix together Coca-Cola and barbeque sauce and pour over chicken pieces. Cover and bake 1/2 hour at 350°. Remove cover. Bake an additional 45 minutes, until tender. Serves four.

TARRAGON CHICKEN

- 2 pounds bone-in chicken breasts with skin
- Salt and pepper
- 2 tablespoons butter
- 2 tablespoons shallots, finely chopped
- 2 teaspoons chopped fresh tarragon
- 1/2 cup dry white wine
- 1/4 cup water

Sprinkle the chicken with salt and pepper. Heat butter in a skillet and add the chicken, skin side down. Cook about 10 minutes until golden brown. Turn and cook about 5 minutes longer. Remove chicken and set aside. Add shallots to the skillet and cook until slightly soft. Add tarragon and wine and stir to dissolve the brown pieces that cling to the bottom of the skillet. Stir in water and return chicken to the skillet, skin side up. Cover and cook for 15 to 20 minutes. Uncover and cook 5 minutes longer, basting often until the chicken is tender and glazed.

TRISH'S CHICKEN ROLL-UPS

- 6 slices beef (in jar)
- 6 boneless chicken breasts, halved and pounded
- 6 slices bacon
- 1 (10-3/4 ounce) can cream of mushroom soup
- 1 cup sour cream

Rinse beef to remove excess sodium and then pat dry. Pound chicken to flatten. Roll flattened chicken breasts with beef inside. Wrap with bacon and secure with tooth picks. Place in casserole. Mix soup and sour cream thoroughly and spread over chicken. Bake uncovered for three hours at 275°. Serves six.

A long-time family favorite that makes a pleasing presentation for a dinner party. Adding sliced, fresh mushrooms to the sauce really adds a nice flavor. We like to serve this with homemade mashed potatoes and boiled fresh peas.

The following marinades are delicious and packed with flavor!

We always rinse the chicken, pat dry, and trim the fat before using in a recipe.

Mom's tip for chicken: *The real secret to tender chicken breasts is to pound them to an even thickness before marinating or using in your favorite recipe.*

My husband Dan, the grill chef at our cottage, advises to grill chicken until juices run clear.

KEY LIME MARINADE

Key Lime is not only great with chicken, but also packs a flavorful punch with shrimp.

- 2 tablespoons soy sauce
- 2 tablespoons honey
- 2 tablespoons vegetable oil
- 4 tablespoons key lime juice
- 2 teaspoons garlic, chopped

> **Directions for Marinades**
>
> Mix marinade ingredients well and pour into a plastic sealable bag. Add the prepared chicken pieces and marinate, refrigerated, for at least an hour. Several hours or overnight is optimal.
>
> Remember to turn the bag occasionally.

LEMON-BASIL MARINADE

- 2/3 cup olive oil
- 2/3 cup parmesan cheese
- 1/2 cup fresh lemon juice
- 1/3 cup fresh basil
- 1 tablespoon lemon zest
- 3/4 teaspoon salt
- 1/2 teaspoon pepper

> *Mom's tip for marinade: Always keep a bottle of your favorite Italian dressing on the pantry shelf. When time is short or ingredients sparse, use the dressing for a marinade and then grill the chicken. It is superb!*

HONEY-LEMON MARINADE

- 1/4 cup lemon juice
- 1/2 cup dry white wine
- 1 tablespoon honey
- 2 tablespoons olive oil
- 1/4 teaspoon pepper
- 1/4 cup rosemary, thyme, and parsley, combined
- 2 tablespoons lemon zest

FISH & SEAFOOD

Nothing says "summer treat" more than white fish and perch fresh from the Great Lakes. We enjoy preparing and serving fish and seafood dishes. These are some of our favorite shared recipes. Thanks friends!

BAKED LAKE MICHIGAN WHITE FISH OR MICHIGAN TROUT

BARBARA'S FRIED PERCH

ERIC'S KICKIN' SHRIMP

FABULOUS SHRIMP

FILLET OF SOLE WITH MUSHROOMS

HERB-GLAZED SALMON

MARTHA'S FAVORITE FISH TACOS

MUSTARD-DILL BAKED SALMON

SANDY'S SHRIMP TOAST

SEAFOOD QUICHE

SESAME GINGER SALMON

SLOW-ROASTED LEMON-GINGER SALMON

STUFFED SOLE

TILAPIA DIJON

TUNA SANDWICHES

BAKED LAKE MICHIGAN WHITE FISH OR MICHIGAN TROUT

2 pounds white fish or trout
1/2 cup green onions and tops, chopped
1 cup sour cream
1/2 teaspoon salt
Dash of dill weed
1/2 cup Parmesan cheese

Place white fish or trout in well-buttered baking dish. Combine all remaining ingredients except cheese and pour over fish. Bake in a preheated oven at 350° for 20 to 25 minutes. Sprinkle cheese over top and turn broiler on just long enough to brown the cheese lightly. Four servings.

BARBARA'S FRIED PERCH

Perch fillets
Flour
Salt and pepper
Egg, slightly beaten
Bread crumbs, boxed and ready to use
Butter

Mix flour with salt and pepper in a shallow dish. Put beaten egg in a second shallow dish, and bread crumbs in a third dish. Dredge fish in flour, making sure all sides are covered. Dip in beaten egg, and finally, in bread crumbs. Place on a plate in a single layer. Heat butter until hot. Carefully add fillets to the pan and sauté for a couple of minutes on each side, until golden brown. Remove from the frying pan and set on a plate lined with paper towel to help absorb extra butter. Serve with tartar sauce.
Mom's tip: *Make this once and be prepared to make it again and again.*

ERIC'S KICKIN' SHRIMP

4   medium garlic cloves, finely chopped
1/4   pound salted butter, divided
2   tablespoons Sriracha sauce
6   Key limes or 4 Persian limes
Salted water
1-1/2 - 2   pounds raw shrimp, extra-large or jumbo (deveined with shells on)
Chopped fresh cilantro

Gently sauté garlic in 3-tablespoons of the butter, stirring constantly for 2 - 3 minutes. Add Sriracha sauce and remaining butter and juice from limes a little at a time until incorporated. Remove from heat. Bring well-salted water to boil, add shrimp and cook only till the shrimp are opaque. Drain. Place shrimp in large bowl. Pour sauce over shrimp, stir and top with cilantro.

FABULOUS SHRIMP

4 ounces butter
1 lemon
1 packet dried Italian seasoning
1 pound fresh shrimp, shelled and deveined

Melt butter in a baking pan. Slice one lemon and layer it on top of the butter. Place the shrimp on top and sprinkle the Italian seasoning on top. Bake in oven at 350° for 15 minutes.

FILLET OF SOLE WITH MUSHROOMS

1/4 cup chopped onion
2 cups sliced fresh mushrooms
1 tablespoon vegetable oil
2 pounds fillet of sole
1-1/2 teaspoons salt
1/8 teaspoon lemon pepper
1 tablespoon fresh chopped parsley

Sauté onion and mushrooms in oil until onion is lightly browned. In heavy skillet, place fillets in layers with onions and mushrooms between and over the fish. Sprinkle with salt, pepper, and parsley. Simmer covered for 20 minutes. Serves six.

HERB-GLAZED SALMON

1/2 cup apricot preserves
3 tablespoons chopped fresh basil
2 tablespoons butter
4 salmon fillets (4-5 ounces each)
Salt and pepper to taste

Microwave preserves, basil, and butter until butter melts; mix well. Spread one-half of the glaze on salmon; season with salt and pepper to taste. Grill five minutes or until fish begins to turn opaque. Turn the salmon, brush with remaining glaze, and grill until fish flakes easily. For baking, set temperature at 400°. Bake each side for about ten minutes. Serves four.

MARTHA'S FAVORITE FISH TACOS

Dinner at Martha's cottage is always a treat. She served these tacos one night and we have been fans ever since. So, from our cottage to hers... thank you, Martha!

1 cup dark beer
1 cup flour
1 teaspoon salt
1-1/2 pounds skinned white fish or perch fillets
Vegetable oil
12 to 16 corn tortillas, warmed
Cabbage and Cilantro Slaw
Chipotle Tartar Sauce
Lime wedges

Whisk beer, flour, and salt until well blended. Rinse fish and pat dry. Cut into one-inch wide strips. Heat on stove, about one inch of vegetable oil to 360°. Dip fish in beer batter and pan fry until golden brown, two to four minutes per batch. Drain on paper towel and keep warm in 200° oven. Warm the tortillas by wrapping in a kitchen towel and microwaving about one minute.

Cabbage and Cilantro Slaw – Mix all ingredients together and chill until serving time.
10 ounces finely shredded cabbage
1/3 cup chopped fresh cilantro
3 tablespoons lime juice
2 tablespoons vegetable oil
1/4 teaspoon red chili flakes
Salt to taste

Chipotle Tartar Sauce – Mix all ingredients until smooth
1-1/2 tablespoons chipotle chilies
1 cup mayonnaise
1/4 cup sweet pickle relish
1/4 cup chopped white onion

To assemble
Top each tortilla with fish followed by the Cabbage and cilantro Slaw. Serve with Chipotle Tartar Sauce and lime wedges.

MUSTARD-DILL BAKED SALMON

1/2 cup bottled honey mustard dressing
2 tablespoons chopped fresh dill
1 (10 ounce) bag matchstick-cut carrots
1-1/2 pounds salmon fillets, without skin
1/8 teaspoon salt
1/8 teaspoon black pepper
1 (10 ounce) box plain couscous mix

Heat oven to 450°. Prepare a 9x13-inch glass pan with cooking spray. In small bowl, mix dressing and dill. Reserve 4-tablespoons for fish. Add carrots to remaining dressing and toss; place in baking dish. Season salmon fillets with 1/8-teaspoon salt and 1/8-teaspoon black pepper. Place salmon on top of carrots. Spoon 1-tablespoon of reserved dressing mixture over each piece of salmon. Bake for 15 to 18 minutes or until salmon is cooked through. While salmon is cooking, prepare couscous following package directions, omitting oil. Serve salmon and carrot mixture over cooked couscous.

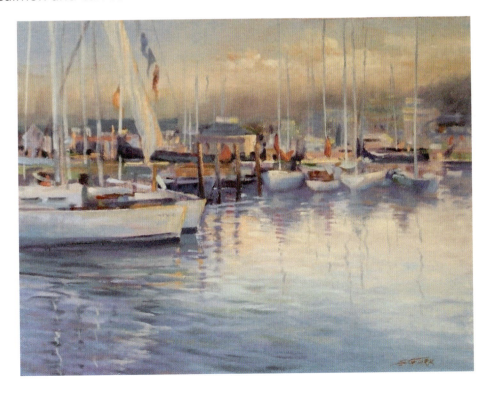

SANDY'S SHRIMP TOAST

1 cup cooked shrimp
1/4 cup minced scallions
4 tablespoons mayonnaise
2 eggs, hard boiled and chopped
1/4 teaspoon ground black pepper
6 slices buttered toast
1/2 cup grated Parmesan cheese

Chop shrimp and blend in scallions, mayonnaise, eggs, and pepper. Heap on toast squares, sprinkle with cheese, and broil for a few minutes until lightly browned. Serve with fresh sliced Michigan tomatoes for a light and delicious meal.

SEAFOOD QUICHE

1/4 cup minced onion
2 tablespoons butter
1 tablespoon tomato paste
1/4 cup red wine
1 pound shrimp
1 pound crabmeat
2 tablespoons parsley
2 tablespoons chives
Dash cayenne pepper
1 pie shell
1-1/4 cups Gruyere cheese, shredded
1 cup whipping cream
1/2 cup half & half
5 large eggs
1/2 teaspoon basil
1/4 teaspoon fennel seeds
Salt and pepper to taste

Sauté onion in butter. Stir in tomato paste. Add wine and cook until down to 2-tablespoons. Add shrimp and cook until pink. Add crab meat, parsley, chives, salt, and pepper. In pie shell, add the meat mixture and top with cheese. Mix together whipping cream, half & half, eggs, basil, fennel seeds, cayenne, salt, and pepper. Pour over meat and cheese. Bake at 375° for 40 - 45 minutes, or until firm.

Serve quiche with a fresh fruit salad and hot dinner rolls. This combination is perfect for a summer evening dinner or a brunch with friends.

SESAME GINGER SALMON

- 1/4 cup olive oil
- 2 tablespoons soy sauce
- 2 tablespoons rice vinegar
- 2 tablespoons sesame oil
- 2 tablespoons brown sugar
- 2 cloves garlic, pressed
- 1 tablespoon grated fresh ginger
- 1 tablespoon sesame seeds
- 4 green onions, thinly sliced
- 4 salmon fillets

In a medium bowl whisk together all ingredients except the salmon fillets. Place the fillets and the marinade in a plastic bag. Marinate for at least one hour or overnight, turning the bag occasionally.

<u>Honey Ginger Glaze</u> – Wisk together all ingredients

- 2 tablespoons honey
- 1 teaspoon soy sauce
- 1 teaspoon sesame oil
- 1/2 teaspoon Sriracha, or more, to taste
- 1/2 teaspoon grated fresh ginger
- 1/2 teaspoon sesame seeds

To bake, preheat oven to 400° and lightly coat a 9x13-inch baking dish with nonstick spray. Place salmon fillets with the marinade into the baking dish. Bake until the fish flakes easily with a fork, about 20 minutes. Brush the honey ginger glaze on top of the salmon and serve immediately.

SLOW-ROASTED LEMON-GINGER SALMON

Roasting a whole salmon fillet on a bed of chard leaves adds flavor and moisture to the fish while eliminating the need to cook the fillet with the skin on. The chard, infused with the flavor of the lemon-ginger glazed fish, can also be served as a tasty side dish. Low-heat roasting keeps the fish moist and silky, but be careful not to overcook it. The fish is done when the flesh barely starts to separate or flake as you gently press it.

4 to 6 leaves from one small bunch rainbow or red Swiss chard, stems removed
2 pounds salmon fillet, skin removed
1/2 teaspoon coarse sea salt
1/4 teaspoon pepper
3 tablespoons honey
2 teaspoons grated lemon peel, divided
1 teaspoon lemon juice
1/2 teaspoon grated fresh ginger
3 tablespoons green onions, sliced

Heat oven to 275°. Line large rimmed baking sheet with foil; lightly spray with cooking spray. Arrange chard leaves down center of baking sheet in a shape slightly larger than the salmon. Place salmon on top of chard; sprinkle with salt and pepper. Bake 20 minutes. Meanwhile, combine honey, 1-teaspoon of the lemon peel, lemon juice, and ginger in small bowl. Spoon over salmon. Bake an additional five to ten minutes or until salmon begins to flake. Serve whole salmon fillet on large platter or cut into serving pieces; sprinkle with green onions and remaining one teaspoon lemon peel. Coarsely chop chard and serve alongside salmon. Serves eight.

STUFFED SOLE

2 tablespoons butter
1/2 teaspoon seasoned salt
1 teaspoon lemon juice
1/4 teaspoon horseradish

5 drops Tabasco sauce
1/3 cup heavy whipping cream
1 can crab or 1/2 pound fresh crab
4 fillets of sole

Topping
1/4 cup of melted butter
1 tablespoon fresh parsley

1 teaspoon lemon juice
1 teaspoon lemon zest

Melt butter and then stir in salt, lemon juice, horseradish, and Tabasco. Blend in cream. Bring to a boil, stirring constantly. Remove from heat, add the crab, and set aside. Butter a baking dish and layer two fillets on the bottom. Next add crab mixture and top with two remaining fillets. Combine all topping ingredients and pour over fillets. Refrigerate for at least one hour. Bake at 350° for 30 minutes.

TILAPIA DIJON

4   (6 ounce) tilapia fillets
1/2   teaspoon salt
1/2   teaspoon pepper
4   tablespoons butter, divided
1/2   cup Dijon mustard
4   tablespoons chopped fresh parsley
2   tablespoons grated lemon zest
1   cup panko
1/2   cup grated Parmesan cheese

Sprinkle fish with salt and pepper. Melt 1-tablespoon of the butter. Combine melted butter, mustard, parsley, and lemon peel in a small bowl. Spread over both sides of tilapia. Combine panko and cheese in shallow dish and generously coat tilapia with crumbs. Melt remaining 3-tablespoons butter in large nonstick skillet over medium-high heat. Cook tilapia 8 to 10 minutes or until it just begins to flake, turning once. Garnish with slices of fresh lemon.

TUNA SANDWICHES – *Open faced and broiled!*

1   small can tuna
English muffins
2-3   tablespoons mayonnaise
1   teaspoon Dijon mustard
1   tablespoon onion, finely chopped
Salt and pepper to taste
Tomato slices
Cheddar or American cheese, sliced

Set oven to broil. Drain tuna. Lightly toast English muffin halves. Meanwhile, mix tuna, mayonnaise, mustard, onion, salt, and pepper until well blended. Spread tuna mixture on toasted English muffins and top with a slice of tomato. Add the cheese on the top of sandwich, place on a baking sheet and put under the broiler until sandwich warms and cheese is bubbly, approximately 3 to 4 minutes.

PASTAS

Nothing says "comfort food" more than a good pasta dinner. And actually, nothing is as comforting as gathering together with family and friends to share stories of the day on Mackinac Island.

BAKED OR GRILLED CHICKEN WITH ANGEL HAIR PASTA

BAKED TURKEY ZITI

CAVATAPPI WITH GRILLED CHICKEN & ASPARAGUS

CHICKEN & BROCCOLI ALFREDO

CHICKEN LASAGNA

CHICKEN PASTA PARMESAN

CHICKEN TETRAZZINI

CORNED BEEF CASSEROLE

CREAMY CLAM SPAGHETTI

EASY LASAGNA

MARINARA & MEATBALLS

GRANDMA'S MACARONI & CHEESE

PARMESAN LINGUINI

SAUSAGE & MACARONI CASSEROLE

SEAFOOD LASAGNA

SHRIMP SCAMPI

SHRIMP THERMIDOR

SO EASY FRESH TOMATO SAUCE

SPAGHETTI CARBONARA

VEGGIE LASAGNA

ZESTY PARMESAN PASTA

BAKED OR GRILLED CHICKEN WITH ANGEL HAIR PASTA

6 skinless, boneless chicken breast halves
4 tablespoons butter
1 envelope Italian dressing mix
1/2 cup white wine (Chardonnay)
1 (10-3/4 ounce) can golden mushroom soup
4 ounces cream cheese with chives
1 pound angel hair pasta

This recipe is thanks to our friend, Pat, who has three boys and knows how to "feed them happy!" For a variation we like to grill chicken and serve it sliced on top of the pasta and sauce. Paired with a fresh tossed salad, it's a winner!

In large pan, melt butter over low heat. Add package of dressing mix. Blend in wine and undiluted can of soup. Blend in cream cheese and stir until smooth, heating thoroughly. Arrange chicken in baking dish. Pour sauce over. Bake at 325° for 60 minutes. Serve with angel hair pasta cooked according to directions on package. Serves six.

BAKED TURKEY ZITI

1 pound ziti pasta
1 onion, chopped
1 pound ground dark turkey
1 teaspoon garlic salt
2 (26 ounce) jars spaghetti sauce
8 ounces provolone cheese, sliced
1-1/2 cups sour cream
8 ounces mozzarella cheese, shredded
4 tablespoons grated Parmesan cheese

Cook pasta according to directions. Drain. Brown onion, turkey, and garlic salt over medium heat. Add spaghetti sauce and simmer 15 minutes. In buttered casserole pan, layer 1/2 of the ziti, provolone cheese, sour cream, 1/2 of the sauce, remaining ziti, mozzarella cheese, and remaining sauce. Top with grated Parmesan cheese. Bake at 350° for 30 minutes or until cheeses are melted. Serves six to eight.

CAVATAPPI WITH GRILLED CHICKEN & ASPARAGUS

1/2 cup extra-virgin olive oil
2 tablespoons sherry vinegar or red wine vinegar
3 large garlic cloves, minced
3/4 teaspoon salt
1/4 teaspoon pepper
4 chicken breast halves, boneless and skinless
1 pound asparagus
8 ounces cavatappi (corkscrew pasta)
2 cups halved small cherry tomatoes
3/4 cup freshly grated Parmesan cheese, divided
1/2 cup chopped fresh basil

My husband Dan does the grilling while the rest of us sit around and watch! He grills everything with great success on an antique charcoal grill. Not sure we would know what to do with a gas grill!

Heat grill. Whisk oil, vinegar, garlic, salt, and pepper in small bowl. Reserve 1/3 cup of the dressing; brush remaining dressing over chicken and asparagus. Grill asparagus, covered, over medium heat or coals 4 minutes or until crisp-tender, turning once. At same time, grill chicken 8 to 10 minutes or until no longer pink in center, turning once. Place chicken on cutting board; cover loosely with foil. Let stand 5 minutes. Slice chicken; cut asparagus into 1-1/2 inch pieces. Meanwhile cook cavatappi according to package directions, drain. Heat reserved dressing in same pot over medium heat. Add cavatappi and tomatoes and toss to coat. Stir in chicken and asparagus. Add 1/2 cup of the cheese and basil and toss. Sprinkle with remaining 1/4 cup cheese. Serves four to six.

Although this calls for chicken, we like to occasionally use shrimp instead. Boil, sauté, or grill the shrimp and use it in place of the chicken.

CHICKEN & BROCCOLI ALFREDO

8 ounces linguine
1 cup broccoli flowerets
2 tablespoons butter
1 pound chicken breasts cut into 1-1/2 inch pieces
1 (10-3/4 ounce) can cream of mushroom soup
1/2 cup milk
1/2 cup grated Parmesan cheese
1/4 teaspoon ground black pepper

Cook linguine according to directions. Add broccoli during last four minutes of cooking time. Drain well. Heat butter in 10" skillet. Add chicken and cook until well browned, stirring often. Mix soup, milk, cheese, pepper, and linguine mixture into skillet. Cook mixture until hot and bubbling. Serve with additional Parmesan cheese. Serves six.

CHICKEN LASAGNA

> We appreciate any lasagna recipe that calls for uncooked noodles. This saves preparation time and it works!

Sauce
1/2 cup chopped onion
1 (28-ounce) can diced tomatoes with juice
1/4 cup bottled salsa
1 envelope taco seasoning mix
1 (16-ounce) can black beans

Ricotta Filling
1 large egg
1-1/2 cups ricotta cheese
2 garlic cloves, minced

Lasagna
10 uncooked lasagna noodles
4 boneless chicken breast halves, cooked and cut bite size
1 (4 ounce) can chopped green chilies
2-4 cups shredded cheese (cheddar, Monterey Jack, or mozzarella)

Combine sauce ingredients and set aside. For ricotta filling, stir egg enough to break yolk. Add egg and garlic to ricotta and mix until blended.

Cover bottom of pan with sauce and top with half the noodles. Place half of the chicken, green chilies, and sauce over noodles. Spoon on ricotta mixture and spread evenly. Add half the shredded cheese. Cover cheese with the rest of the noodles, and add remaining chicken, chilies, and sauce. Top with cheese.

Bake at 350° for 40 minutes covered. Uncover and bake 20 minutes more. Let it set for 15 to 20 minutes before cutting. Serves six to eight.

CHICKEN PASTA PARMESAN

1 pound chicken or turkey breast, boneless and skinless
2 tablespoons vegetable oil
1/2 pound mushrooms
1/4 cup chopped onion
2 tablespoons dry sherry
1 (10-3/4 ounce) can cream of chicken soup
1/2 cup thinly sliced red and green peppers
1/2 cup grated Parmesan cheese
1 pound linguine

In skillet, cook chicken until browned in hot oil. Remove, cut in bite-sized pieces and set aside. In drippings, cook mushrooms and onion until tender. Add sherry and soup. Heat thoroughly, stirring often. Add chicken and peppers. Cover. Simmer for 10 minutes, stirring occasionally. Stir in cheese until melted. Serve over hot cooked pasta. Serves four.

CHICKEN TETRAZZINI

1 pound thin spaghetti
2 (10-3/4 ounce) cans mushroom soup
1 soup can of milk
1 pound fresh mushrooms, sautéed several minutes
1 tablespoon Worcestershire sauce
3 tablespoons sherry
1/2 teaspoon each onion salt and garlic salt
6 chicken breasts, pounded and cut in large pieces
10 ounces sharp cheese, grated
Dash pepper and paprika

Cook spaghetti al dente. In a bowl, mix together soup, milk, mushrooms, Worcestershire sauce, sherry, and salt. Alternate in layers in large casserole: half of spaghetti, half of chicken, half of soup mixture, and half of cheese. Repeat. Sprinkle with paprika and pepper. Bake at 350° covered for 30 minutes, then uncovered for an additional 30 minutes. Serves six.

CORNED BEEF CASSEROLE

1 cup celery, sliced
1/2 cup onion, chopped
1/2 cup green pepper, chopped
1 (8 ounce) package noodles, cooked & drained
1 can corned beef, chopped
1/4 pound Velveeta cheese
1 (10-3/4 ounce) can cream of mushroom soup
1 cup milk
Bread crumbs
Butter

Cook vegetables until tender. Combine vegetables with noodles, corned beef, cheese, soup and milk and place in a 9x12 greased casserole. For that special crunchy texture add bread crumbs and dabs of butter on top. Bake 40 minutes at 350°. Serves eight.

CREAMY CLAM SPAGHETTI

8 ounces fresh mushrooms
2 cloves garlic
1/2 cup butter
6 tablespoons flour
4 cans chopped clams, drained (reserve liquid)
2 cups cream
1/2 cup plus grated fresh Parmesan cheese
2 tablespoons sherry
2 tablespoons parsley
1/2 teaspoon pepper
Linguini

Flavorful pasta recipes are on the top of our list after a day of Mackinac Island outdoor activity. It's easy to work up an appetite biking to Wawashkamo Golf Club to enjoy an afternoon of golf and comradery. Wawashkamo is open to the public so be sure to schedule a round when you visit the Island.

Cook mushrooms and garlic in butter. Gently stir in flour. Gradually stir in clam liquid and cream and stir until thick. Add and thoroughly heat the clams, 1/2-cup cheese, and the remaining ingredients. Serve over hot linguini with freshly grated Parmesan cheese on the side. Serves six.

EASY LASAGNA

1 pound ground beef or Italian sausage
4 cups tomato-basil pasta sauce
6 uncooked lasagna noodles
1 (15 ounce) container ricotta cheese
1-1/2 cups shredded mozzarella cheese
1/4 cup hot water

Cook meat over medium heat until done; drain. Stir in pasta sauce. Spread one-third sauce in lightly greased baking dish; layer with three noodles, half of ricotta cheese, and half of mozzarella cheese. Repeat procedure; spread remaining one-third of meat sauce over mozzarella cheese. Slowly pour 1/4-cup hot water around inside edge of dish. Tightly cover baking dish with two layers of heavy duty aluminum foil. Bake at 375° for 45 minutes; uncover and bake ten more minutes. Let stand ten minutes before serving. Serves six.

MARINARA & MEATBALLS – *Eric's original*

2 tablespoons olive oil
1 large sweet pepper, finely diced (red, yellow, or orange)
1 large onion, finely diced
2 stalks celery, finely diced
3 - 4 pounds ground beef
8 large cloves of garlic, minced
1 tablespoon fennel seed crushed, divided
2 tablespoons basil, divided
2 teaspoons oregano, divided
2 teaspoons red pepper flakes, divided
2 tablespoons fresh chopped parsley, divided
3 - 4 pounds ground beef
3 eggs, whipped
3 handfuls grated Pecorino Romano cheese
3 handfuls seasoned bread crumbs
2 teaspoons salt
1 teaspoon black pepper
2 bay leaves
4 (28 ounce) cans of crushed tomato (if desired, add additional chopped tomatoes)

Optional: 16-ounces fresh mushrooms, cut in quarters, and 1/2-cup red wine. Add to sauce with meatballs.

Meatballs Method
Preheat oven to 325°.
Heat 2 tablespoons olive oil in large skillet. Sauté sweet peppers, onion, and celery until soft. Add garlic, 1/2-tablespoon fennel seed, 1-tablespoon basil, 1-tablespoon oregano, 1-teaspoon red pepper flakes, and 1-tablespoon parsley and sauté an additional 2 minutes. Place 2/3 of sautéed mixture in large mixing bowl and allow to cool. Add ground beef,

3 whipped eggs, cheese, breadcrumbs, salt, pepper, and 1 teaspoon pepper flakes. Mix thoroughly with hands. Line 2-3 jelly roll pans with parchment paper. Form meatballs to desired size and place in oven until cooked through (20 to 30 minutes based on size). Allow to cool while sauce is prepared.

Sauce Method
Place remaining sautéed mixture in large pot on low heat. Add crushed tomatoes, remaining 1-tablespoon basil, 1-teaspoon oregano, 1/2-tablespoon crushed fennel seed, 1-teaspoon salt, bay leaves, 1-teaspoon red pepper flakes, and heat to simmer.

Wipe meatballs with paper towel and add to sauce (if desired, add mushrooms and wine at this time). Allow mixture to simmer for 30 to 40 minutes. Taste and add additional salt, basil, and red pepper flakes as may be needed.

Serve over spaghetti.

GRANDMA'S MACARONI & CHEESE

This is the best ever macaroni and cheese. Everyone in our family makes it, carrying on Grandma's great cooking legacy. Since we like to keep kitchen time to a minimum, Mom and I have taken a few time-saving liberties. We use shredded extra-sharp cheddar and mix everything together before putting into a baking dish. Our last dab of yummy is to top the casserole with more cheese and add bread crumbs drizzled with melted butter.

1 pound box macaroni
2 plus pounds cheddar cheese
Milk

Cook macaroni according to box instructions. Cut cheese in 1/2-inch squares and cut a few slices for topping. Alternate macaroni and cheese in buttered casserole. Cover with cheese slices and pour milk into the casserole until it is almost to the top of the macaroni. Bake approximately one-half hour at 350° until it is heated through and top cheese is lightly browned.

PARMESAN LINGUINI

- 1 tablespoon olive oil
- 4 cloves garlic, minced
- 2 cups chicken broth
- 1 cup milk, or more as needed
- 2 tablespoons unsalted butter
- 8 ounces uncooked linguini
- Sea salt and freshly ground black pepper to taste
- 1/4 cup freshly grated Parmesan cheese
- 2 tablespoons chopped fresh parsley leaves

Heat olive oil in a large skillet over medium high heat. Add garlic and cook, stirring frequently, about 1 to 2 minutes. Stir in chicken broth, milk, butter, and linguini; season with salt and pepper to taste. Bring to a boil. Reduce heat and simmer, stirring occasionally, until pasta is cooked through, about 8 minutes. Stir in Parmesan. If the mixture is too thick, add more milk as needed until desired consistency is reached. Serve immediately, garnished with fresh parsley.

SAUSAGE & MACARONI CASSEROLE

2 pounds Bob Evans sausage
1 large onion, chopped
1 cup green pepper, chopped
4 (14 ounce) cans diced tomatoes
4 tablespoons Worcestershire sauce
2 tablespoons chili powder
2 teaspoons Italian seasoning
Water
2 cups elbow macaroni
2 cups grated cheddar cheese

Mom can whip this up in no time at all, which is a good thing, especially on busy days. On several occasions, and to everyone's delight, we have taken it to our neighbor's backyard barbecue potluck. There are never leftovers!

Brown sausage, onion, and green pepper. Stir in tomatoes, Worcestershire sauce, chili powder, Italian seasoning, and water (up to one cup, if needed). Bring to boil, simmer 15 minutes. Cook macaroni according to directions. Mix macaroni and shredded cheese with meat mixture, place in large casserole and bake at 350° for one hour. Serves eight.

SEAFOOD LASAGNA

- 8 lasagna noodles
- 1 cup chopped onion
- 2 tablespoons butter
- 8 ounces cream cheese, softened
- 1-1/2 cups cottage cheese, cream style
- 1 egg, beaten
- 2 teaspoons basil
- 1/2 teaspoon salt
- 1/4 teaspoon pepper
- 2 cans cream of mushroom soup
- 4 ounce jar sliced mushrooms, drained
- 1/3 cup milk
- 1/3 cup dry white wine
- 1 (7-1/2) ounce can crabmeat
- 1 pound salad shrimp
- 1/3 cup Parmesan cheese
- 1 cup shredded mozzarella cheese

Heat oven to 350°. Cook noodles as directed on package, drain. Place four noodles in greased 9x13x2-inch baking dish.

In saucepan, cook onions in butter until tender. Blend in cream cheese. Stir in cottage cheese, egg, basil, salt, and pepper. Spread half of mixture over noodles in pan.

In medium bowl, combine soup, mushrooms, milk, and wine. Stir in crab and shrimp, and spread half of the mixture over cottage cheese layer.

Repeat layers. Sprinkle with Parmesan cheese. Bake uncovered for about 45 minutes. Top with mozzarella cheese. Bake till cheese begins to brown. Let stand for 10 minutes before serving.

SHRIMP SCAMPI

1/4 cup olive oil
1 cup fresh mushrooms
1 pound peeled and deveined large shrimp (raw, 20 to 25 per pound)
4 large garlic cloves, left unpeeled and forced through a garlic press
1/2 cup dry white wine
1 teaspoon salt
1/2 teaspoon black pepper
5 tablespoons unsalted butter
3/4 pound capelli d'angelo (angel-hair pas
1/2 cup fresh flat-leaf parsley, chopped
Parmesan cheese, freshly grated

Heat oil in a 12-inch heavy skillet over moderately high heat until hot, but not smoking. Add mushrooms and then shrimp. Sauté until until cooked through, turning over once, about 2 minutes. Transfer with a slotted spoon to a large bowl.

To the oil remaining in the skillet, add garlic, wine, salt, and pepper. Cook over high heat for one minute, stirring occasionally. Add butter to skillet, stirring until melted. Stir in shrimp and mushrooms. Remove from heat.

Cook pasta in boiling water until just tender (don't overcook). Reserve 1 cup of pasta-cooking water, then drain pasta. Toss pasta well with shrimp mixture and parsley in large bowl. Add some of the reserved cooking water if necessary to keep moist. Serve Parmesan cheese on the side. Serves six.

SHRIMP THERMIDOR

1/4 cup butter
1-1/2 cups mushrooms, sliced
1/2 cup green onion, chopped
1/4 cup flour
1 teaspoon salt
1/8 teaspoon ground red pepper
1/2 teaspoon dry mustard
2 cups half & half
1-1/2 pounds shrimp, peeled, deveined, and cooked
1/4 cup Parmesan cheese, freshly grated
Paprika
1 pound linguini

Preheat oven to 400°. Melt butter in medium skillet over medium heat. Add mushrooms and green onions; sauté five minutes. Whisk in flour, salt, pepper, and mustard. Gradually add the cream and continue whisking constantly, about five minutes, until sauce is thickened. Stir in cheese. Bake for 10 minutes until bubbly. Add cooked shrimp and heat another 5 minutes. Cook and drain linguini according to directions. Spoon the hot shrimp mixture over linguini. Serve freshly grated Parmesan on the side.
Add a fresh loaf of French bread and a green salad to complete your menu.

This is one of mom's extraordinary recipes. It is easy to make and definitely worthy of a main dish presentation at any special dinner party.

SO EASY FRESH TOMATO SAUCE

2 cups fresh tomatoes
1 tablespoon olive oil
2 large clove garlic, minced
1 tablespoon fresh basil, snipped
Salt and pepper to taste
6 ounces pasta
Parmesan cheese, fresh grated

Mix first 5 ingredients together and let set for a couple of hours. Cook and drain pasta of your choice and add to room-temperature-tomato mixture. Serve Parmesan cheese on side.

SPAGHETTI CARBONARA

10 bacon strips, cooked and crumbled
2 eggs, slightly beaten
1 cup Parmesan cheese, grated
1/4 cup cream
Salt and pepper, to taste
1 (16 ounce) package spaghett

Combine all ingredients except spaghetti. Cook pasta and drain. Toss spaghetti with the bacon mixture and serve immediately. Serves four to six.

Mom's Tip: *The least messy way to cook bacon is to use the oven. Spread bacon slices on a baking sheet and roast at 325° for 30 minutes, turning occassionally. Adjust time to reach desired doneness. No more splatters!*

VEGGIE LASAGNA

1 (10 ounce) package chopped spinach
1 (16 ounce) package ricotta cheese
1-1/2 cups shredded mozzarella
1 egg
3/4 teaspoon oregano
Salt and pepper to taste
1 (32 ounce) spaghetti sauce
1 package lasagna noodles, uncooked
1 cup water

Thaw and drain spinach. Mix ricotta, 1-cup mozzarella, egg, spinach, oregano, salt, and pepper together. Set aside. Vegetable Spray 9x13 pan. Layer 1-cup sauce on bottom. Cover with noodles and 1/2 of the cheese mixture. Repeat two more times using 1/2-cup sauce. Top with 1/2-cup mozzarella. Pour one cup water around edges. Cover with foil and bake 1 hour 15 minutes at 350°. Uncover last 10-15 minutes to brown. Let stand before serving.

ZESTY PARMESAN PASTA

1 cup olive oil
1-1/4 cups freshly grated Parmesan cheese
3/4 cup fresh lemon juice (about two lemons)
1/2 teaspoon salt, plus more to taste
1/4 teaspoon freshly ground black pepper
1 pound angel hair pasta
1/2 cup fresh basil, chopped
Zest from 2 lemons
Pine nuts, toasted

Mix oil, Parmesan cheese, lemon juice, 1/2-teaspoon salt, and 1/4-teaspoon pepper to blend. Set the lemon sauce aside. Meanwhile bring a large pot of water to boiling. Add pasta and cook according to directions until tender. Drain, reserving one cup of the cooking liquid. Add pasta to the sauce and toss with the basil, lemon zest, and toasted pine nuts. Toss pasta with enough cooking liquid to moisten. Season with more salt and pepper to taste. We recommend serving extra cheese with the pasta. **So easy, so yummy!**

SIDE DISHES

"Action" is the best descriptive for the beautiful harbor. There is always something different and new to see!

ADDY'S MARVELOUS MUSHROOMS

ALSATIAN ONION TART

ASPARAGUS & BLUE CHEESE

ASPARAGUS BUNDLES

ASPARAGUS WITH TOMATOES

BAKED PINEAPPLE

BRUSSEL SPROUTS

CHEESY BROCCOLI CASSEROLE

CHEESE-FROSTED CAULIFLOWER

CORN SPOON BREAD

COWBOY SLOW COOKER BEANS

FLYING HIGH MASHED POTATOES

FOUR-CHEESE SCALLOPED POTATOES

GARLIC-TOASTED ASPARAGUS

GREEN BEANS & PORTABELLO

MUSHROOMS SAUTÉ

GREEN BEANS WITH BROWNED BUTTER

OLD ENGLISH ASPARAGUS CASSEROLE

PARMESAN MASHED POTATOES

POTATOES SUPREME

ROASTED BRUSSEL SPROUTS WITH PANCETTA & SAGE

ROASTED POTATOES & VEGGIES

SAUSAGE STUFFING BALLS

SCALLOPED POTATOES

SPINACH & MUSHROOM CASSEROLE

SWEET POTATO CASSEROLE

SWEET POTATOES WITH APPLES

SQUASH SOUFFLE

VEGGIE CASSEROLE

WHITE MOLD

ZUCCHINI AU GRATIN

ZUCCHINI CASSEROLE

ADDY'S MARVELOUS MUSHROOMS

1 pound fresh mushrooms
1/3 cup butter, softened
1 tablespoon minced parsley
1 tablespoon minced onion
1 tablespoon Dijon mustard
1 teaspoon salt
Pinch of cayenne pepper
1-1/2 tablespoons flour
1 cup heavy cream

Wipe mushrooms clean with damp paper towel and trim stem ends. Place mushrooms in a 1-quart casserole. Mix butter, parsley, onion, mustard, salt, cayenne, and flour. Spread this mixture over top of mushrooms. Pour cream over top and bake uncovered at 375° for 1 hour, stirring a couple of times. This is a wonderful accompaniment to steak or beef roast. Serves four.

ALSATIAN ONION TART

Pastry
3 cups flour
1-1/2 teaspoons salt
Pinch of sugar
3/4 cup chilled butter cut in 1/2 inch pieces
1/2 cup vegetable shortening, chilled
1/4 cup sour cream
1/4 cup cold water (or more)

Sift flour, salt, and sugar together. Add butter and shortening mixing with pastry blender until it looks like coarse meal. Blend sour cream with water. Add to flour mixture; stir gently with a fork. Add more water if necessary to have dough form a ball. Roll into 8x12-inch rectangle on floured surface. Fold in thirds, like a letter. Rotate dough 1/4 turn. Repeat rolling and folding once. Wrap and chill one hour to three days. Roll on floured surface into a 12x17-inch rectangle and fit into a 10x15x1-inch pan. Crimp edges and prick lightly. Chill 20-30 minutes. Put aluminum foil on top of dough and weigh it down with dry beans. Bake for 8 minutes at 400°. Remove weights and foil; prick again and bake until golden brown (10-11 minutes).

Filling
8 ounces bacon, cut in 1/2-inch pieces
2 tablespoons unsalted butter
2-1/2 pounds, onions, halved lengthwise and cut into 1/4-inch pieces
1/4 cup flour
Salt and pepper
1-1/4 cups milk
4 eggs
3/4 cup whipping cream
1/8 teaspoon grated nutmeg
1/8 teaspoon ground red pepper

Cook bacon over low heat until browned. Remove bacon with slotted spoon and set aside. Add butter to skillet. Add sliced onion, tossing to coat. Cover and cook, stirring occasionally, until soft, not brown. Sprinkle with flour, stir three to four minutes. Add bacon and season lightly with salt and pepper. Spread into baked crust. Whisk milk, eggs, and cream to blend. Season with nutmeg and red pepper. Pour evenly over onion mixture. Bake at 375° for 30 to 35 minutes. Serve warm.

Alsatian Onion Tart is a fabulous side dish; however, the preparation is time consuming. Happily though, the crust can be made up to three days in advance. We love to serve it with steaks or a good roast as the flavor enhances the taste of the meat. It is a real crowd pleaser, especially for onion lovers.

ASPARAGUS & BLUE CHEESE

Asparagus
Blue Cheese Dressing
Red onion, diced

Blanch whole asparagus spears in a large skillet half full of water for a few minutes. Drop into iced water to stop cooking. Arrange spears on platter and drizzle dressing over the center of them. Sprinkle with diced red onion.

Use your favorite recipe for homemade dressing. We, however, always use a prepared Blue Cheese dressing because tasty, quick, and easy is our goal! Golf anyone?!

Side Dishes | 155

ASPARAGUS BUNDLES

2 pounds fresh asparagus, trimmed
12 slices bacon
1/2 cup light brown sugar
1/2 cup butter
1 tablespoon soy sauce
1/2 teaspoon garlic salt
1/4 teaspoon freshly ground pepper

Preheat oven to 400°. Divide the asparagus spears into 12 bundles. Carefully wrap one piece of bacon around each bundle, starting about 1/2-inch from the bottom of the tips. Secure the bacon-wrapped spears with a toothpick. Lay the bundles in a low-sided casserole dish. Combine sugar, butter, soy sauce, garlic salt, and pepper in a medium saucepan. Bring the mixture to a boil. Pour the hot sugar mixture over the asparagus bundles. Roast until the spears have begun to wilt and the bacon looks fully cooked, about 25 minutes. Remove toothpicks before serving.

ASPARAGUS WITH TOMATOES

1 bundle asparagus
1 medium tomato, diced or 1/2 cup cherry tomatoes, cut in half
1/4 cup capers
Balsamic vinegar

Steam asparagus spears for a few minutes, then toss with diced tomato and capers. Drizzle with balsamic vinegar.

BAKED PINEAPPLE

1 cup sugar
2 tablespoons flour
Dash of salt
2 eggs, beaten
1 (20 ounce) can crushed pineapple, undrained
1/2 cup butter
5 slices white bread, cut in cubes, with or without crusts
Maraschino cherries, cut in half for garnish (Optional)

Mix sugar, flour, and salt. Blend eggs and pineapple together and add to dry mixture, mixing well. Pour into greased 8x8-inch baking dish. Melt butter in saucepan, add bread cubes and toss to coat. Sprinkle over pineapple mixture. Garnish with cherries. Bake at 375° for 40 minutes. Recipe may be doubled and will need a few more minutes in the oven.

BRUSSELS SPROUTS

Our family and friends are bacon lovers, so even those who aren't crazy about brussels sprouts love this side dish!

2 pounds brussels sprouts, cut bite-size
4 slices bacon, cut in one-inch pieces
1 tablespoon olive oil
1 large onion, chopped

Freshly ground pepper to taste
1/4 cup balsamic vinegar
1 tablespoon Dijon mustard

Cook brussels sprouts until almost tender in boiling water. Drain. Meanwhile cook bacon in a large heavy-duty skillet over medium heat until brown. Drain on paper towel leaving about 1-tablespoon of bacon fat. Adding oil then onion, cook and stir often until soft and lightly brown. Add brussels sprouts along with pepper, balsamic vinegar, and Dijon mustard stirring occasionally until tender. Serves six.

CHEESY BROCCOLI CASSEROLE

1 (6 ounce) package Stove Top stuffing mix for chicken
2 (10 ounce) packages frozen broccoli florets, thawed, drained
1 (10-3/4 ounce) can cream of mushroom soup
1 cup Cheez Whiz cheese dip

Prepare stuffing mix as directed on package using only 3-tablespoons margarine or butter. Set aside. Mix remaining ingredients in two-quart baking dish; top with stuffing. Bake 30 minutes at 350° until heated through.
Serves four to six.

CHEESE-FROSTED CAULIFLOWER

1 medium head cauliflower
1/2 cup mayonnaise
2 teaspoons prepared mustard
3/4 cup shredded cheddar cheese
Paprika
Tomato wedges
Fresh parsley

Wash cauliflower, remove leaves, and cut out base. Put whole cauliflower in covered pot with boiling water and cook for approximately 15 minutes until tender. Drain and place in an ungreased shallow baking pan. Combine mayonnaise and mustard. Spread Spread over cauliflower and bake at 375° for 5 minutes. Remove from oven, sprinkle with cheddar cheese, and bake an additional 5 minutes. Remove from oven, sprinkle top with paprika and garnish with tomato wedges and fresh snipped parsley.

Quick, easy, and mouthwatering, this Corn Spoon Bread recipe is on our "go to" list. Not only is it a great addition to a barbecue or potluck, it is also perfect to add to your Thanksgiving dinner menu.

CORN SPOON BREAD

2 eggs, slightly beaten
1 (8-1/2 ounce) package Jiffy corn muffin mix
1 (8 ounce) creamed style corn
1 (8 ounce) whole kernel corn
1 cup sour cream
1/2 cup melted butter
1 cup shredded Swiss cheese

Combine all ingredients except the cheese. Spread into a prepared 8x12-inch baking dish or casserole dish. Bake at 350° for 35 minutes. Sprinkle Swiss cheese on top. Bake 10 minutes more, or until knife comes out clean.

COWBOY SLOW COOKER BEANS

6 slices bacon, cut into pieces
3/4 pounds ground beef
2 onions, chopped
1 clove garlic, minced
1 (16 ounce) can baked beans
1 (16 ounce) can kidney beans, drained
1 (15 ounce) can butter beans, drained
2 shots espresso
1/3 cup vinegar
1 teaspoon Worcestershire sauce
1/2 cup brown sugar
1 tablespoon dry mustard

Cook bacon until crisp, drain, and break into small pieces. Lightly brown beef, onions, and garlic in skillet. Drain. Combine all ingredients in slow cooker. Mix well. Cover. Cook on low for 5 to 7 hours, or bake in the oven at 325° for 2 hours.

Side Dishes | 159

FLYING HIGH MASHED POTATOES *is a tried and true recipe from my days as a flight attendant with United Airlines. It is now one of our favorite "go-to" potato recipes.*

FLYING HIGH MASHED POTATOES

8-10 potatoes
8 ounces sour cream
1/2 cup butter
4 ounces cream cheese
8 ounces cheddar cheese, shredded
Milk as needed

Peel and boil potatoes until tender. Beat potatoes, sour cream, and butter until smooth. Stir in cream cheese and cheddar cheese last. IMPORTANT: do not beat the potatoes while adding cream cheese and cheddar because it will adversely affect the texture. Use milk as needed to thin. Top with cheddar cheese. Bake at 350° until heated through and cheese has melted.

FOUR-CHEESE SCALLOPED POTATOES

1-1/2 tablespoons butter, cut into pieces plus more for brushing
1/2 clove garlic
1/3 cup shredded mozzarella cheese
2/3 cup Mexican blend cheese
2 pounds russet potatoes, peeled and sliced 1/8 inch thick
Salt and freshly ground pepper
2 cups heavy cream
1/4 teaspoon freshly grated nutmeg
4 fresh bay leaves
1/4 cup grated Parmesan cheese

Preheat oven to 425°. Generously brush a large skillet with butter, then rub with the garlic. Combine mozzarella and Mexican cheese. Heat skillet over medium-high heat. Add half of the potatoes, spreading them out. Sprinkle with 3/4-teaspoon salt, half of the cut-up butter, half of the cheese blend and pepper to taste. Arrange remaining potatoes on top. Sprinkle with 3/4-teaspoon salt and pepper to taste. Pour the cream over the potatoes, then add the nutmeg and bay leaves. Simmer three minutes. Dot the potatoes with the remaining cut-up butter.

Bake in skillet, if oven-proof. If not, slide potatoes into a prepared casserole dish. Sprinkle with Parmesan and the remaining cheese blend. Bake about 25 minutes until golden. Let rest for five minutes before serving. Discard the bay leaves. Serves six to eight.

Side Dishes

GARLIC-TOASTED ASPARAGUS

- 2 pounds asparagus, tough ends trimmed, rinsed, and patted dry
- 3 tablespoons extra-virgin olive oil
- 1-1/2 tablespoons minced garlic
- Salt (to your taste)
- Freshly ground black pepper
- 2 teaspoons fresh lemon juice

In a large glass baking dish, toss the asparagus with the olive oil and garlic. Season lightly with salt and pepper and toss. Bake at 400° until the asparagus' are tender and lightly browned, about 25 minutes, stirring twice. Sprinkle with lemon juice.

GREEN BEANS & PORTOBELLO MUSHROOM SAUTÉ

1-1/4 pounds green beans, trimmed and cut in half
1/8 teaspoon salt
2 tablespoons extra-virgin olive oil
1 tablespoon butter
1 onion, chopped
2 Portobello mushroom caps, halved and thinly sliced
Salt and pepper
1/2 cup dry sherry

Mom's tip: Chopping onions is not my favorite activity. Therefore, I always chop two at a time, one for the current recipe and the other to put in a small Baggie and freeze for a future recipe.

Simmer green beans in salted boiling water five minutes. Drain and set aside in a bowl. Add oil and butter to the pan over medium heat. Add onion and sauté two to three minutes. Add mushrooms and season with salt and pepper. Sauté mushrooms three to five minutes with onions. Add green beans and heat through. Then add sherry and cook for one to two minutes. Serves six.

GREEN BEANS WITH BROWNED BUTTER

3/4 pound fresh green beans
2 tablespoons butter (Do not use margarine)
2 tablespoons pine nuts
1 teaspoon grated lemon zest

Fresh from the garden vegetables are such a treat! Everyone finishes their green beans when we serve them browned butter style!

Heat beans in water to boiling. Reduce heat and simmer till tender. Melt butter in saucepan over low heat and stir in pine nuts. Continue cooking, stirring constantly, until butter is golden brown. Immediately remove from heat. Pour butter mixture over beans and toss to coat. Sprinkle with lemon zest and serve at once. Serves six.

OLD ENGLISH ASPARAGUS CASSEROLE

2 (15-ounce) cans asparagus spears
1/2 cup sliced almonds
2 tablespoons butter
2 tablespoons flour
1-1/2 cups milk
1 (5 ounce) jar Kraft Old English cheese spread
Dash salt
Dash red pepper
1-1/2 cups crackers crushed
1/2 cup melted butter.

Arrange asparagus in buttered pan and sprinkle with almonds. Melt two tablespoons butter in heavy saucepan over medium heat. Stir in flour. Gradually add milk, stirring until sauce thickens. Add cheese and stir until melted. Season with salt and pepper. Pour sauce over asparagus. Combine cracker crumbs with 1/2-cup butter. Sprinkle over casserole. Bake 350° for 20-30 minutes. Serves six.

PARMESAN MASHED POTATOES

3 pounds potatoes, peeled and cut into chunks
3 bay leaves
4 ounces butter, cut into chunks
2 cups shredded Parmesan
1/2 cup heavy cream
Salt and pepper to taste
1/4 cup chopped fresh chives

Boil the potatoes with the bay leaves until tender. Drain well and discard the bay leaves. Mash the potatoes, then stir in chunks of butter and cheese. Let stand until butter and cheese melts. Stir in the cream, season with salt and pepper. Beat until creamy. Fold in chopped chives. Serves six to eight.

POTATOES SUPREME

4 ounces butter, melted and divided
1 (30 ounce) frozen hash brown potatoes
1 (10-3/4 ounce) can cream of chicken soup
1 medium onion, grated, or 1/3 cup green onions, sliced
8 ounces sour cream
1/4 teaspoon salt
1/4 teaspoon black pepper
1 cup shredded cheddar cheese
1 cup corn flakes, crushed

Pour melted butter over frozen hash browns. (Save two tablespoons for topping). Add soup, onion, sour cream, salt and pepper to the hash browns and place in a large prepared rectangular casserole dish. Sprinkle cheese over top. Melt two tablespoons of butter and mix with crushed corn flakes. Sprinkle on top of cheese. Bake for one hour at 350°.

ROASTED BRUSSELS SPROUTS WITH PANCETTA & SAGE

1 large leek, thinly sliced, white and light green parts
2 pounds brussels sprouts, trimmed and halved (about 8 cups)
1/2 cup chopped pancetta (2 ounces)
2 tablespoons fresh sage, finely chopped
2 tablespoons extra-virgin olive oil
1/2 teaspoon salt
1/2 teaspoon freshly ground pepper

Preheat oven to 450°. Combine leek with sprouts, pancetta, sage, oil, salt, and pepper in roasting pan. Roast, stirring once, until sprouts are tender, about 18 to 20 minutes. Serves eight.

ROASTED POTATOES & VEGGIES

We take many liberties with this recipe by adding whatever vegetables we have on hand. Adjust the olive oil mixture for the amount of vegetables you are roasting.

- 8 small potatoes, cleaned and cut in half
- 8 ounces fresh mushrooms
- 2 onions, pealed and cut in quarters
- 1/4 cup olive oil
- 4-6 cloves garlic, crushed
- 1 tablespoon fresh rosemary or chives, chopped

You, too, can experiment with a variety of seasonal fresh vegetables to create the perfect side dish for your special dinner.

Combine all vegetables in a large bowl and toss with a mixture of olive oil, garlic, and rosemary to coat well. Pour into a shallow baking dish and bake at 350° until tender and brown, approximately 30 to 40 minutes. If you prefer, grilling the seasoned veggies is a great option.

SAUSAGE STUFFING BALLS

- 1 (8 ounce) brown and serve sausage
- 1-1/2 cups blanched almonds, chopped
- 2 eggs
- 1/2 cup water
- 1 (16 ounce) package bread stuffing
- 3/4 cup ripe olives, sliced

Finely chop sausage and sauté in pan for two to three minutes. Add almonds and sauté two minutes longer. Remove from heat. Beat eggs and water together and add to stuffing. Add sausage, almonds, and olives. Shape into 2-1/2-inch balls. Place on greased baking sheet and bake uncovered 25 minutes at 325°.

SCALLOPED POTATOES

2 tablespoons unsalted butter
1 small onion, finely chopped
4 cloves garlic, minced
1 tablespoon flour
Salt and pepper
3 cups half-&-half
2 to 3 teaspoons paprika
2-1/2 pounds russet potatoes, peeled and thinly sliced
1 cup shredded cheddar cheese
1/3 cup freshly grated Parmesan cheese

Preheat oven to 350°. Spray a 9x13 casserole dish with vegetable oil. Melt the butter in large sauce pan. Add onions and garlic and sauté until softened, about four minutes. Add in order, the flour, salt, pepper, half-&-half, paprika, and potatoes. Bring to a low simmer and cook for five minutes.

Pour half of the potato mixture into the prepared casserole dish. Sprinkle half of each of the cheeses on top. Add remaining potatoes and arrange in a layer. Sprinkle on remaining cheese. Cover with foil and bake for 50 minutes or until bubbling. Remove foil and bake for another 15 minutes or until the potatoes are tender and cheese is nicely browned. Let stand for 5 minutes before serving.

Mom Tip: To save time, check your local market for pre-sliced potatoes which are usually found in the refrigerated section. However, be sure to make this recipe even if you have to slice them yourself. It will be a favorite for all potato lovers.

SPINACH & MUSHROOM CASSEROLE

2 (10 ounce) packages frozen chopped spinach
1/2 pound fresh mushrooms, sliced
2 tablespoons butter
4 slices American cheese, diced
1 (12 ounce) can evaporated milk
1/4 teaspoon garlic powder

Cook spinach according to package directions. Drain thoroughly. Sauté mushrooms in butter. Melt cheese in milk in a heavy pan over low heat. Turn spinach into a shallow baking dish. Sprinkle with garlic powder; stir in cheese mixture. Top with mushrooms and drippings. Bake uncovered at 350° for 20 minutes.

SWEET POTATO CASSEROLE

3 cups cooked sweet potatoes
6 ounces butter, melted, divided
1 (14 ounce) can sweetened condensed milk
3/4 cup brown sugar
Pecan pieces

Using a mixer, beat together potatoes, 4-ounces butter, and the milk. Place mixture in an oiled baking dish. Stir together the brown sugar and remaining melted butter. Place on top of the potatoes and sprinkle with pecan pieces. Bake at 350° for 30 to 40 minutes.

SWEET POTATOES WITH APPLES

4 apples
1/2 cup brown sugar
1/2 teaspoon nutmeg
1/2 cup butter, divided

4 sweet potatoes, cooked and mashed
1 teaspoon salt
1/2 teaspoon pepper
Butter for top of casserole

Peel, seed, and chop apples. Place in buttered casserole. Mix brown sugar, nutmeg, and 1/4- cup butter together and spread over apples. Mix sweet potatoes with salt, pepper, and 1/4-cup butter. Place over apple mixture. Dot casserole with butter. Bake at 375° for 45 minutes.

Side Dishes

SQUASH SOUFFLE

2 packages frozen squash, cooked
4 tablespoons butter
2 tablespoons brown sugar
1/2 teaspoon salt
1/2 teaspoon orange zest
1/8 teaspoon ground nutmeg
Dash of pepper
4 eggs, separated

Combine squash, butter, brown sugar, salt, orange zest, nutmeg, and pepper in a large bowl. Beat until fluffy. Add egg yolks and beat again. In a cold metal bowl, beat eggs whites until stiff peaks form. Fold the egg whites into the squash mixture and pour into an oven safe 6-cup soufflé dish. Bake at 350º for 55 to 60 minutes.

VEGGIE CASSEROLE – *Nancy's best!*

6 medium tomatoes
6 medium potatoes
6 medium zucchinis
Caramelized onions*
Olive oil
Parmesan cheese

Slice potatoes, tomatoes, and zucchini about 1/4-inch. In a prepared casserole, place one slice each of potato, tomato, and zucchini on end in a row. Repeat pattern, making three rows. Cover with caramelized onions. Drizzle with olive oil, cheese, salt, and pepper. Bake at 350° until tender, about 30 minutes.

*Caramelized Onions
2 large onions
3 tablespoons olive oil or butter
Salt and pepper to taste

Cut onions in half and then make slices about 1/4-inch thick. Heat oil and/or butter in frying pan. Add onions, cover and cook on low heat for about ten minutes. Uncover, turning heat up to low medium, and stirring often until brown. Add more oil if necessary.

WHITE MOLD – *It tastes so much better than its name suggests!*

8 ounces cream cheese
1 large bag marshmallows
1/2 cup milk
1 large container small curd cottage cheese
1 large Cool Whip
1 small can pineapple, drained

We love to serve this side dish. It's just fun to list it on the menu!

Have cream cheese at room temperature. Melt marshmallows in hot milk. Let cool. Whip cream cheese, cottage cheese, Cool Whip, and pineapple. Whip it into the cooled marshmallow mixture and turn into a 9x13-inch pan. Refrigerate overnight.

ZUCCHINI AU GRATIN

3 tablespoons butter
1/4 cup onions, chopped
2 pounds zucchini, sliced or cut in chunks
4 tomatoes, sliced
1 cup mozzarella or cheddar cheese, cubed
1/2 teaspoon salt
1/8 teaspoon pepper
1/2 cup buttered toasted bread crumbs

Heat butter in frying pan and sauté onions. Add zucchini, cook for about 5 minutes. Layer zucchini and onions in buttered baking dish with tomatoes and cheese, adding seasonings. Top with bread crumbs. Bake at 350° for about 25 minutes. Serves six.

ZUCCHINI CASSEROLE

2 pounds zucchini
1 medium onion, chopped
2 carrots, grated
1 (10-3/4 ounce) can cream of chicken soup
1 cup sour cream
4 ounces butter
1 (8 ounce) package Pepperidge Farm Stuffing

Thanks to our good friend Hannah, this tasty zucchini dish is prepared every summer as a special treat. She loves to spoil us with her personal, always delicious, favorite recipes! She knows how to keep us smiling!

Cook zucchini with onions and carrots until tender (do not overcook) and drain well. Blend soup and sour cream; add to veggies. Mix butter with stuffing. Put half of the stuffing mix in a 9x13-inch pan; add zucchini mix and top with remainder of stuffing. Bake for 20 minutes at 350° until bubbly.

DESSERTS

My husband Dan gave each of our three daughters their very first flower, a Forget-Me-Not! This tiny, delicate flower blankets many areas of the Island in the early season and brings us happy and sweet memories.

- APPLE CAKE WITH GLACE
- APPLE & CRANBERRY CRISP
- APPLE PIE WITH SALTED CARAMEL
- BANANA SPLIT DESSERT
- BANANA & STRAWBERRY TRIFLE
- BARBIE'S BUTTERSCOTCH CHOCOLATE CAKE
- BROWNIE REFRIGERATOR CAKE
- CHERRY PIE
- CHOCOLATE HEATH TRIFLE
- COCA-COLA CAKE
- CRANBERRY POUND CAKE WITH HOT CARAMEL SAUCE
- EAST BLUFF STRAWBERRY SHORTCAKE
- FROZEN PUMPKIN ICE CREAM PIE
- GLORIOUS DUMP CAKE
- GINGERBREAD CAKE
- HEAVENLY ORANGE-PINEAPPLE CAKE
- HOT FUDGE SAUCE
- ICE CREAM PIE WITH CARAMEL SAUCE
- JO'S DESSERT
- KAHLUA CHOCOLATE CAKE
- KEY LIME PIE
- LEMONADE CHEESECAKE
- LEMON CAKE
- LEMON DELIGHT
- LEMON SAUCE
- LUSH LEMON FROSTING
- PEACH DUMPLINGS
- PEANUT BUTTER PIE (EASY)
- PIE CRUST
- PINEAPPLE ANGEL FOOD CAKE
- PINEAPPLE FRUIT CAKE
- PUMPKIN CHIFFON
- PUMPKIN DESSERT
- PUMPKIN PIE
- PUMPKIN PIE CAKE
- PUMPKIN PIE – TURTLE STYLE
- RHUBARB CRISP
- ROCKY'S CARAMEL CAKE
- STEPHANIE'S BLUEBERRY BUCKLE
- STRAWBERRY TORTE
- TEXAS SHEET CAKE WITH FROSTING

APPLE CAKE WITH GLACE

3 cups flour
1 teaspoon salt
2 cups sugar
1 teaspoon baking soda
2 teaspoons vanilla plus 1/4 teaspoon
1-1/2 cups oil
3 eggs
2 cups chopped apples
1-1/4 cups chopped pecans
4 ounces butter
1/2 cup brown sugar

Mix flour, salt sugar, and baking soda together. Combine two teaspoons vanilla, oil, and eggs. Add to the dry mixture, mixing well. Fold in apples and nuts. Bake in a Bundt pan at 325° for one hour 20 minutes. Boil the butter, sugar, and 1/4-teaspoon vanilla on medium heat for two minutes. Pour over cake while hot.

APPLE & CRANBERRY CRISP

4 medium cooking apples, peeled and sliced
1 teaspoon cinnamon
1 (13 ounce) can whole cranberry sauce
1 cup uncooked quick oats
1/2 cup flour
1 cup dark brown sugar
1/2 cup butter

Arrange apples in 10-inch baking dish. Sprinkle with cinnamon. Spoon cranberry sauce over apples. Mix oats, flour, and brown sugar together; cut in butter until crumbly. Sprinkle over cranberry layer. Bake at 350° for 40 minutes. Serve with whipped cream or ice cream.

APPLE PIE WITH SALTED CARAMEL – *Libby's Specialty!*

The men in our family LOVE pie (who doesn't?). We started making this apple pie (recipe adapted from Four and Twenty Blackbirds) when we discovered how much fun it is to bake while talking with family and visiting friends. The bottom line is, we don't have an apple corer nor mandolin in our cottage kitchen! So, preparing the apples for this pie requires at least two sets of hands and a lot of chit chat.
The surprising thing about this recipe is that even with all that caramel, the end result is not too sweet. Remember: homemade crust is a must!

Pastry for a two-crust pie

<u>Salted Caramel</u>
1 cup white sugar
1/4 cup water
1/2 cup unsalted butter
1/2 cup fresh heavy cream
1-1/2 teaspoons sea salt

Cook sugar and water over low heat until just dissolved. Add butter and bring to a slow boil. Continue cooking at a low boil until the mixture turns a deep, golden brown color, almost copper. This process takes a while. Keep watch and don't let the caramel smoke. Remove from heat and add the heavy cream. The mixture will bubble and steam. Whisk the mixture together well over low heat and sprinkle in the sea salt. Set aside.

<u>Apple Pie Filling</u>
4 to 6 lemons
5 to 6 medium to large apples
1/3 cup raw sugar
2 tablespoons flour
1/4 teaspoon ground cinnamon
1/4 teaspoon ground allspice
1/8 teaspoon freshly grated nutmeg
2 to 3 dashes bitters

Juice lemons into a large bowl. Core, peel, and thinly slice the apples. Dredge apples in lemon juice and set aside. In a small bowl, combine sugar, flour, cinnamon, allspice, nutmeg, and bitters. Sprinkle over the apples. Gently mix with your hands to coat slices.

Assembling
1 egg, well beaten
Raw sugar for sprinkling on top
1 teaspoon sea salt (flake)

Layer 1/3 of the apples in the bottom of the crust so that there are minimal gaps. Pour 1/3 of the caramel over the apples. Repeat two more times. Save a small portion of the caramel to pour on top once the lattice is assembled and fluted. Brush lattice with beaten egg and lightly sprinkle with raw sugar and sea salt. Bake in a 400° oven for approximately 45 minutes or until apples are tender. **This is fantastic all by itself, but served warm with vanilla ice cream is outrageous!**

BANANA SPLIT DESSERT

2 cups graham cracker crumbs
4 ounces melted butter
4 ounces softened butter
2 cups powdered sugar
2 eggs
4-6 bananas cut lengthwise
1 (13 ounce) can crushed pineapple (drained)
1 (15 ounce) carton Cool Whip (fluffed a little)
3/4 cup nuts, chopped
Maraschino cherries

Mix graham cracker crumbs with 4-ounces melted butter and press in 9x13-inch pan. Chill one hour. Beat the softened butter, powdered sugar, and eggs for ten minutes. Spread on crumb mixture. Layer the bananas, crushed pineapple, Cool Whip, and nuts. Maraschino cherries may be placed on each serving or chopped and sprinkled over top.

BANANA & STRAWBERRY TRIFLE

1 angel food loaf cake, cut in chunks
1 (3.4 ounce) box instant banana pudding mix
Milk according to pudding mix directions
4 medium size bananas, cut in thick slices
1 carton fresh strawberries, cut in half
1 (15 ounce) can chunk pineapple, drained
1 (15 ounce) Cool Whip

Place 1/2 angel food cake chunks in bottom of large glass bowl. Mix pudding mix according to directions. Cover the cake chunks with 1/2 pudding. Layer with 2 bananas and 1/2 of the pineapple chunks. Cover with 1/2 Cool Whip. Add layer of strawberries. Repeat the layers, chill, and serve.

BARBIE'S BUTTERSCOTCH CHOCOLATE CAKE

1 chocolate cake mix
1 jar butterscotch topping
8 ounces Cool Whip, thawed
3 (2.1 ounce) Butterfinger candy bars, coarsely crushed

Prepare and bake cake in a 9x13-inch pan following directions on the box. Cool on rack for 30 minutes. Poke twelve holes in warm cake using a wooden spoon handle. Pour butterscotch topping over cake and cool completely. Spread with whipped topping and sprinkle with crushed candy. Refrigerate for at least two hours before serving.

Our love of cooking is really a love of togetherness with family and friends. It is heartwarming to watch our daughters working in the kitchen together as they create a scrumptious dessert. Libby made a beautiful wedding cake for Katie and Josh. Barbie and friend Jamie made the dessert for Katie's rehearsal dinner. The rest of us enjoyed their efforts. What lovely memories!

BROWNIE REFRIGERATOR CAKE

1   box brownie mix
1   extra large egg
8   ounces cream cheese, softened
1   cup powdered sugar
2   (8 ounce) containers whipped topping
1   (3-3/4 ounce) package instant chocolate pudding
1   (3-3/4 ounce) package instant vanilla pudding
3-1/2 cups milk
1   Hershey candy bar or chocolate syrup

Mix brownie mix according to directions adding one egg and bake in a 9x13-inch pan. Mix cream cheese, powdered sugar, and one container whipped topping. Put this mix on top of the cooled brownies. Blend puddings and milk together and put on top of the cream cheese mixture. Top with another layer of whipped topping. Put chocolate shavings or chocolate syrup on top. Refrigerate until ready to serve.

CHERRY PIE

1-1/3 cups sugar
4   tablespoons quick-cooking tapioca
1/2   teaspoon cinnamon
Pinch of salt
4   drops almond flavoring
4   cups pitted sour cherries
1-1/2   tablespoons butter
Pastry for a two-crust 9-inch pie

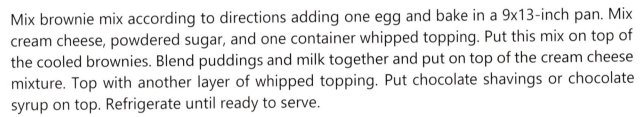

Mix dry ingredients. Stir lightly into cherries. Add almond flavoring and mix. Place in your favorite pie shell. Dot with butter. Cover with slotted top crust. Seal and flute. Bake 35-45 minutes at 425°. Serve warm or cold with vanilla ice cream.

CHOCOLATE HEATH TRIFLE

1 chocolate cake mix
2 (5.1 ounce) boxes instant chocolate pudding—not sugar free
2 cups coffee-flavored liqueur
2 cups milk
2 (12 ounce) containers Cool Whip
1 (8 ounce) package Heath Bits

Bake chocolate cake as directed. Break cake into large pieces and place half in a large clear glass bowl or a 9x13-inch pan. Mix pudding as directed on box using liqueur for 1/2 of the milk. Spread half of pudding over cake layer. Top with half of Cool Whip and place half of the Heath Bits over the Cool Whip. Repeat layers. Top with remaining candy.

Picnics, potlucks, porch parties, and backyard barbecues are a big part of every Mackinac Island summer season. Coca-Cola cake is a quick and easy recipe that is perfect for any occasion. It is moist, scrumptious, and sure to please all chocolate lovers!

Mom's tip: *If you don't keep buttermilk on hand, there is an emergency substitution! Add one tablespoon of lemon juice or vinegar to a cup of milk and let set for five to ten minutes. Stir it and use it for any baking recipe that calls for buttermilk.*

COCA-COLA CAKE

- 2 cups flour
- 2 cups sugar
- 1 cup butter
- 3 tablespoons cocoa
- 1 cup Coca-Cola
- 1/2 cup buttermilk
- 2 eggs
- 1 teaspoon baking soda
- 1 teaspoon vanilla
- 1-1/2 cup miniature marshmallows

Combine flour and sugar in large bowl. In small saucepan, heat 1-cup butter, 3-tablespoons cocoa, and 1-cup Coca-Cola. Bring to simmer and pour over flour mixture. Stir well. Add buttermilk, eggs, baking soda, and vanilla to flour mixture. Mix well and fold in marshmallows. Pour into a prepared 9x13-inch pan. Bake for 35 minutes at 350°.

Frosting
- 3 cups powdered sugar
- 3 tablespoons cocoa
- 1/2 cup butter
- 6 tablespoons Coca-Cola

Place powdered sugar in a bowl. Bring the butter, cocoa, and Coca-Cola to a boil in a saucepan. Pour the mixture over the powdered sugar. Beat well. Spread evenly over warm cake. Cool and serve.

CRANBERRY POUND CAKE WITH HOT CARAMEL SAUCE

3 cups flour
1/2 teaspoon baking soda
1/2 teaspoon salt
1 cup butter, softened
2 cups sugar, divided

6 large eggs, separated
2 teaspoons vanilla extract
8 ounces sour cream
2 cups fresh or frozen cranberries

Preheat oven to 350°. Grease and flour a Bundt pan. Sift together flour, soda, and salt. Cream together butter and 1-3/4-cups sugar at medium-high speed until light and fluffy. Add egg yolks, two at a time, beating just until blended after each addition. Add vanilla and beat until well blended. Add flour mixture to butter mixture, alternately, with cream, beating at low speed, ending with flour mixture.

Beat egg whites on high speed until foamy. Gradually add remaining 1/4-cup sugar, beating until stiff peaks form. Fold one-third of the egg whites into cake batter. Fold in remaining egg whites, then fold in the cranberries. Spoon into a pound-cake pan and bake at 350° for one hour or until an inserted tester comes out clean. Cool in the pan on wire rack for ten minutes.

<u>Sauce – to be served over pound cake</u>
1 cup brown sugar, firmly packed
1 cup heavy cream
4 tablespoons butter
1 cup white sugar

Combine all ingredients and boil, stirring constantly until sugar dissolves, 3 to 5 minutes. Serve the sauce over slices of pound cake.

For an easier time beating egg whites, we use a cold metal bowl. Freeze the bowl and metal beaters for a few minutes, add egg whites, and beat away! Another great tip from Barbara. Thanks Mom!

This recipe began many years ago when my in-laws summered at the cottage. They had become friends with Michigan's then Governor, G. Mennen "Soapy" Williams, and family. One sunny July day, a casually dressed governor brought a flat of ripe summer berries to the cottage for a birthday party. The housekeeper, not recognizing him, told him to take his delivery around back to the kitchen door. As the story goes, the governor did just that and with a smile on his face. That story always comes up when we serve this dessert.

EAST BLUFF STRAWBERRY SHORTCAKE

2 quarts strawberries
1/4 to 1/2 cup sugar
2 cups all-purpose flour
5 teaspoons baking powder
1 teaspoon salt
2 tablespoons sugar
1/4 cup shortening
2/3 cup milk
Butter for spreading on bottom half
Whipped cream or Cool Whip

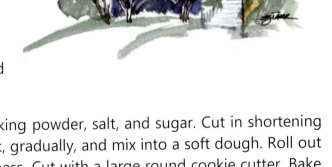

Wash and slice strawberries. Add sugar and let set for an hour.

Preheat oven to 425°. Mix and sift flour, baking powder, salt, and sugar. Cut in shortening with a knife or mix with finger tips. Add milk, gradually, and mix into a soft dough. Roll out on a lightly floured board to 1/2-inch thickness. Cut with a large round cookie cutter. Bake for 15 minutes. Break apart while hot and spread bottom cake with butter.

Spoon sliced berries between and on top of cakes. Serve with whipped cream. This recipe makes eight shortcakes.

FROZEN PUMPKIN ICE CREAM PIE

Pastry for a one-crust pie
1 pint vanilla ice cream, softened
1 (15 ounce) can pumpkin
1-3/4 cups sugar, divided
1/2 teaspoon salt
1 teaspoon cinnamon
1/2 teaspoon ginger
1/4 teaspoon cloves
1 teaspoon vanilla
1 cup whipping cream
1 cup slivered almonds
Additional whipped cream for serving

Prepare your favorite pie crust. On cooled crust, spread one pint softened vanilla ice cream. Freeze. Mix pumpkin, 1-1/2-cups sugar, salt, cinnamon, ginger, cloves, and vanilla. Whip cream until stiff and fold into pumpkin pumpkin mixture. Cover ice cream with mixture. Cover with foil and freeze at least four hours. In the meantime, caramelize the almonds in a small skillet with 1/4-cup sugar over low heat. Stir constantly and rapidly as the sugar begins to turn color. Remove and spread on greased cookie sheet. When cool, break apart. To serve, top each slice with more cream and the almonds.

A favorite for many years, this recipe makes a beautiful presentation and gets many praises whether served with a meal or alone for a dessert offering.

Homemade pie crust is always the best, but when you'd rather be playing putt-putt golf with the kids, use a purchased, ready-made crust. *We won't tell!*

GLORIOUS DUMP CAKE

1 (21 ounce) can cherry pie filling
1 (14.5 ounce) can crushed pineapple, drained
1 yellow cake mix
8 ounces butter, melted
1 cup coconut
1 cup nuts

Prepare a 9x13 baking pan with vegetable spray. Dump all the ingredients in layers as listed above. Bake at 350° for 40 minutes. Cover with foil and bake 10 more minutes.

GINGERBREAD CAKE – *The kind grandma used to make!*

1/2 cup Crisco
1 cup dark brown sugar, packed
2 eggs
1/2 cup barrel molasses
1 teaspoon ginger
1 teaspoon cinnamon
1/2 teaspoon nutmeg
2 cups flour
1 teaspoon baking soda
1/2 teaspoon salt
1/2 cup boiling water

Place shortening and brown sugar in warm bowl and cream together. Beat in eggs and molasses. Add ginger, cinnamon, nutmeg, and one cup flour. Beat hard. Add second cup of flour, baking soda, and salt. Beat one minute by hand. Add boiling water; beat briefly. Bake at 350° for 30 minutes in an 8x12-inch prepared pan. Cake doubles in height while baking. Serve with lemon sauce. (recipe on page 192)

HEAVENLY ORANGE-PINEAPPLE CAKE

1   yellow cake mix
1   (6-1/4 ounce) can mandarin oranges, do not drain
1/2   cup vegetable oil
4   whole eggs, slightly beaten

In a large mixing bowl, blend cake mix, oranges, oil, and eggs with electric mixer. Beat for two minutes on medium speed. Bake at 325° in two greased and floured nine-inch cake pans or a 9x13-inch pan for time recommended on the cake box. When cool, spread with pineapple frosting and refrigerate until served.

Pineapple Frosting
1   (20 ounce) can crushed pineapple in heavy syrup, do not drain
1   (3.4 ounce) vanilla instant pudding
1   (9 ounce) carton whipped topping or one pint whipping cream, whipped

In medium bowl, mix pineapple and pudding until thick. Fold in topping or cream.

HOT FUDGE SAUCE

4   (1 ounce) squares unsweetened baking chocolate
2   tablespoons butter
1/3   cup strong black coffee
1/3   cup boiling water
2   cups sugar
1/4   cup corn syrup
1   tablespoon rum

Melt chocolate in top section of double boiler set over gently simmering water. Add butter and stir until melted. Pour in coffee and water, stirring constantly until well combined. Blend in sugar and corn syrup. Transfer mixture to small saucepan. Cover and boil, without stirring, for three minutes. Reduce heat and cook for two minutes, uncovered, without stirring. Remove from heat and stir in rum. Serve immediately over ice cream.

ICE CREAM PIE WITH CARAMEL SAUCE

1 egg white, room temperature
1/4 cup sugar
1-1/2 cups chopped pecans
1 quart vanilla ice cream, softened
Pecan halves (optional)

Beat egg white with an electric mixer at high speed. Gradually add sugar, one tablespoon at a time, beating until stiff peaks form and sugar dissolves. Fold in chopped pecans. Press mixture on bottom and sides of a buttered 10-inch pie plate. Bake at 400° for 12 minutes or until lightly browned. Cool completely. Spread ice cream evenly over crust. Cover and freeze until ice cream is firm. Garnish with pecan halves. Spoon caramel/raisin sauce over each serving.

Caramel/Raisin Sauce
3 tablespoons butter
1 cup light brown sugar, firmly packed
1/2 cup whipping cream
1/2 cup golden raisins
1 teaspoon vanilla extract

Melt butter in saucepan. Add sugar and cream stirring over low heat until sugar dissolves. Add raisins and vanilla. Stir well.

JO'S DESSERT

1 yellow or lemon cake mix
3 eggs
4 ounces melted butter
8 ounces cream cheese, softened
1 pound box powdered sugar
1 teaspoon vanilla (optional)

Preheat oven to 350°. Grease and flour a 9x13-inch pan. Mix together the cake mix, one egg, and butter until crumbly. Press the mixture into the cake pan for crust. Mix together the cream cheese, sugar, and two eggs until smooth. Add vanilla and mix. Pour over crust and bake for 45 minutes. You may cover with foil if top gets too brown.

KAHLUA CHOCOLATE CAKE

1 devil's food cake mix
4 eggs
1 cup sour cream
1 cup Kahlua
3/4 cup vegetable oil
1 cup semisweet chocolate chips

Combine all ingredients, except chips. Beat three to five minutes with electric mixer. Stir in chips. Pour into greased and floured 10-inch Bundt pan. Bake at 350° for 55-60 minutes. Cool 30 minutes. Loosen the sides and invert on rack. Serve with whipped cream or ice cream.

Kahlua Chocolate Cake is our first choice for a dinner party when preparation time is limited. Serve it warm or at room temperature and top it off with vanilla ice cream or whipped cream. For the final touch of scrumptiousness, drizzle Kahlua over all!

KEY LIME PIE

1 (14 ounce) can sweetened condensed milk
8 ounces cream cheese, softened
1/2 to 3/4 cup juice from key limes
1/2 teaspoon vanilla
1 graham cracker crust (9-inch)
Whipped cream topping

Combine sweetened condensed milk, cream cheese, and key lime juice. Beat on low speed until smooth. Add vanilla to mixture. Pour into crust and refrigerate until set. Top with whipped cream.

Lemons are our favorite ingredient to have on-hand in the good old summertime. From drinks to main courses to desserts, this citrus fruit adds just the right amount of zing to every dish. Lemon dessert recipes are our first choice when we need a light treat after a big dinner.

LEMONADE CHEESECAKE

- 8 ounces cream cheese, softened
- 1 (14 ounce) can sweetened condensed milk
- 1/2 can frozen lemonade concentrate, thawed
- 16 ounces Cool Whip
- 2 (9-inch) graham cracker pie shells

Combine cream cheese, milk, and lemonade in a bowl. Mix well. Fold in Cool Whip. Spoon into pie shells and chill for three hours. The final touch is to garnish with a little lemon zest on top.

LEMON CAKE – *Thanks Hannah!*

1 lemon cake mix
1 (3-3/4 ounce) box lemon instant pudding
3 large eggs
1/2 cup salad oil
1 cup water
1-1/2 cups powdered sugar
1/2 cup fresh lemon juice

Mix all ingredients, except the last two, together. Pour into a prepared 8x12-inch pan and bake for 45 minutes at 350°. While warm, punch holes in cake with fork. Pour glaze (sugar and lemon juice) over cake.

LEMON DELIGHT

1/2 cup butter, melted
1 cup flour
1/2 cup ground nuts
1 cup powdered sugar
8 ounces cream cheese, soften
2 cups Cool Whip
2 (3.4 ounce) boxes instant lemon pudding
3 cups milk

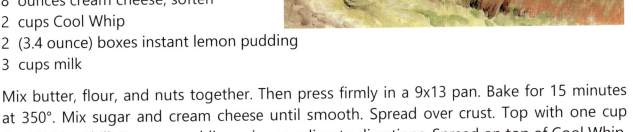

Mix butter, flour, and nuts together. Then press firmly in a 9x13 pan. Bake for 15 minutes at 350°. Mix sugar and cream cheese until smooth. Spread over crust. Top with one cup Cool Whip. Chill. Prepare pudding mix according to directions. Spread on top of Cool Whip. Spread remaining Cool Whip on top of pudding. Chill.

Mom's tip: *make this a chocolate delight! Just replace the lemon pudding with chocolate pudding for a great variation!*

LEMON SAUCE

2 tablespoons cornstarch
1/2 cup sugar
1 tablespoon butter
1 egg
1/8 teaspoon salt
2 cups boiling water
Juice and zest of 1 lemon

Make this delicious topping for gingerbread cake or your favorite, pound cake. Serve it warm and top with a sprinkle of nutmeg.

Mix cornstarch and sugar in saucepan. Add butter, egg, and salt. Beat well. Add boiling water slowly and stir over medium heat until thick. Add lemon juice and zest and remove from heat. Taste and add more lemon juice if needed.

LUSH LEMON FROSTING

8 ounces cream cheese, softened
1/2 cup unsalted butter, softened
1/2 cup lemon curd
2 tablespoons grated lemon peel
4 cups powdered sugar

Beat all ingredients, except sugar, until smooth. Slowly add powdered sugar and beat for two minutes until light and fluffy. Ideal on a lemon cake or try on any of your favorite flavors.

Use this frosting recipe for a quick and easy way to turn a boxed cake mix into a very special dessert.

PEACH DUMPLINGS

2 whole large peaches
2 (8 ounce) cans crescent rolls
8 ounces butter
1-1/2 cups sugar
1 teaspoon vanilla
1-1/2 cups orange juice
Cinnamon, to taste
Ice cream

I will always remember the first time Mom made this dessert. Our girls and their friends had just returned from a bike ride to Arch Rock and were ready for a treat. After the first bite, there was an exclamation heard loud and clear. "Oh wow, I've died and gone to heaven!" We mark this one a huge success!

Peel and pit peaches. Cut both peaches into 8 slices. Roll each peach slice in a crescent roll. Place in a 9x13-inch buttered pan. Melt butter. Add sugar and barely stir. Add vanilla, stir, and pour entire mixture over peaches. Pour orange juice around the edges of the pan. Sprinkle with cinnamon and bake at 350° for 40 minutes. Serve with ice cream, and spoon some of the sweet sauce from the pan over the top.

PEANUT BUTTER PIE – *Easy!*

1 cup crunchy peanut butter
4 ounces cream cheese
1/4 cup powdered sugar
1 (12 ounce) Cool Whip
Crust, your favorite purchased

Cream peanut butter, cheese, and sugar. Add 2/3 of the Cool Whip. Pour into crust. Cool overnight. Cover with remaining Cool Whip before serving.

PIE CRUST

12 tablespoons very cold unsalted butter
3 cups all-purpose flour
1 teaspoon kosher salt
1 tablespoon sugar
1/3 cup very cold vegetable shortening
6 to 8 tablespoons (about 1/2 cup ice water)

Dice the butter and return it to the refrigerator while preparing the flour mixture. Mix dry ingredients together. Add butter and shortening. With fingers fork, or pastry blender, blend until butter is the size of peas. Add ice water gradually and continue mixing until the dough begins to form a ball. Roll into a ball on a floured board. Wrap in plastic and refrigerate for thirty minutes. When ready to fill the pie, cut dough in half and roll each piece on a floured board to fit 9-inch pie pan. Top crust may be slotted or made as a lattice, approximately 1-inch wide.

One of the best things about homemade pie crust is using the scraps to make tarts. Roll the scraps to about a 1/4-inch thickness and cut out circles using a cookie cutter. Use a thimble to cut a small hole in the middle of half of the circles. Bake until light brown. Cool. Add a dollop of jelly or jam to the solid circle and top with the doughnut shaped circle. It's a real treat! **Mom's tip:** *Try Michigan cherry jelly!*

PINEAPPLE ANGEL FOOD CAKE

1 package angel food cake mix
1 (20 ounce) can crushed pineapple (do not drain)
Cool Whip

Mix cake mix and pineapple together. Follow baking instructions on box. Cool completely and top with Cool Whip.

PINEAPPLE FRUIT CAKE

- 1 (20 ounce) can crushed pineapple, do not drain
- 2 cups flour
- 1 cup nuts, broken plus 1/2 cup chopped nuts
- 2 teaspoons baking soda
- 2 cups sugar
- 2 eggs
- 6 ounces cream cheese, softened
- 2 cups powdered sugar
- 6 tablespoons melted butter
- 1 teaspoon vanilla

Mix pineapple, flour, one cup nuts, baking soda, sugar, and eggs in a bowl by hand. Pour into a 9x13-inch prepared baking dish. Bake at 350° for 45 minutes. Meanwhile, thoroughly mix cream cheese, powdered sugar, butter, vanilla, and 1/2-cup nuts. Spread icing on cake while cake is still hot.

A couple of our friends actually grow pumpkins in their summer gardens on Mackinac Island. The results of their efforts are beautiful! So, with all that inspiration, we love to prepare desserts and breads with pumpkin.

Good friends of ours have been known to have a late summer turkey dinner party with all the trimmings as a way to celebrate Thanksgiving with summer friends. So, we think pumpkin is perfect for any time!

PUMPKIN CHIFFON

1-3/4 cups graham cracker crumbs or ginger snap crumbs
1/4 cup sugar
1/2 cup butter, melted
8 ounces cream cheese, softened
2 eggs, beaten
3/4 cup sugar
2 (3-3/4 ounces) packages vanilla instant pudding mix
3/4 cup milk
2 cups pumpkin
1 teaspoon cinnamon
1/2 teaspoon nutmeg
8 ounces frozen whipped topping, thawed
1/2 cup chopped pecans

Combine first three ingredients. Press into a 13x9-inch baking dish. Set aside. Combine cream cheese, eggs, and 3/4-cup sugar. Beat until fluffy. Spread over crust. Bake at 350° for 20 minutes. Set aside to cool. Combine pudding mix and milk. Beat two minutes at medium speed with electric mixer. Mixture will be very thick. Add pumpkin, cinnamon, and nutmeg. Beat until smooth. Fold in one cup whipped topping. Spread pudding mixture over cream cheese layer. Spread remaining whipped topping over pudding layer. Sprinkle top with pecans. Store in refrigerator. Serves twelve.

PUMPKIN DESSERT

- 1 (15 ounce) can pumpkin
- 1 cup brown sugar
- 1 cup white sugar
- 1 can evaporated milk
- 3 eggs
- 1 white or yellow cake mix
- 1-1/2 teaspoons cinnamon
- 1 teaspoon nutmeg
- 1/4 teaspoon cloves
- 1/2 cup butter
- Nuts

Spray 9x12-inch pan. Mix all ingredients except butter and nuts. Pour into pan. Spoon melted butter over cake mixture and top with nuts. Bake at 350° for 50 minutes. Cut into squares.

PUMPKIN PIE – *Grandma Griffes' Special*

Most people think of pumpkin pie for Thanksgiving, but Grandma's recipe is so good that we make it in the summer too! We've never had a complaint!

- 1 large can pumpkin
- 1-1/2 cups sugar
- 5 eggs
- 3 tablespoons molasses
- 1-1/2 teaspoons cinnamon
- Pinch of salt
- 1-1/2 teaspoons ginger
- 2 cups milk
- 1 tablespoon flour

Mix pumpkin, sugar, eggs, and molasses until well blended. Stir dry ingredients together and add to pumpkin mixture. Pour into two pie crusts. Bake at 400° for 55 minutes. **Grandma always said to insert a knife near the middle of the pie. If it comes out clean, it's done!**

PUMPKIN PIE CAKE

4 eggs, slightly beaten
2 (15 ounce) cans solid pack pumpkin
1-1/2 cups sugar
1 teaspoon salt
2 teaspoons cinnamon
1 teaspoon ginger
1/2 teaspoon cloves
3 cups evaporated milk
1 yellow cake mix
4 ounces melted butter
1 cup chopped nuts
Whipped cream

Preheat oven to 350° (glass 325°). Grease 9x13-inch, or slightly larger, pan. Beat eggs. Add pumpkin, sugar, salt, spices, and milk. Pour into greased pan. Sprinkle dry cake mix evenly over top. Drizzle with butter. Sprinkle nuts on top. Bake one hour and fifteen minutes. Cool. Top with whipped cream and serve.

PUMPKIN PIE – TURTLE STYLE

1/2 cup caramel ice cream topping plus 1 tablespoon, divided
1 graham cracker piecrust or regular pastry crust
1/2 cup pecan pieces plus 2 tablespoons, divided
1 cup cold milk
2 (3.4 ounce) French vanilla instant pudding
1 cup canned pumpkin
1 teaspoon ground cinnamon
1/2 teaspoon ground nutmeg
1 (9 ounce) Cool Whip, thawed

Pour 1/4-cup caramel topping onto crust and sprinkle with 1/2-cup pecans. Beat milk, instant pudding mixes, pumpkin, and spices with a whisk until blended. Stir in 1-1/2-cups Cool Whip. Spread on top of pecans layer. Refrigerate at least one hour. Just before serving, top with remaining Cool Whip, caramel topping, and pecan pieces.

RHUBARB CRISP

1 cup light brown sugar, firmly packed
1 cup flour
3/4 cup quick-cooking oats
1/2 cup melted butter
1 teaspoon cinnamon

1 cup granulated sugar
2 tablespoons cornstarch
1 cup water
1 teaspoon vanilla
4 cups rhubarb, cut in bite-size pieces

Mix brown sugar, flour, quick-cooking oats, butter, and cinnamon together. Press 1/2 of the crumb mixture into 8x8-inch pan. Combine sugar, cornstarch, water, and vanilla in saucepan. Cook over medium heat, stirring constantly, until mixture is clear. Add rhubarb to crust and pour sauce over top. Top with remaining crumb mixture and bake at 350° for 45-55 minutes.

ROCKY'S CARAMEL CAKE

1 German chocolate cake mix
1 (8 ounce) package caramels
1/2 cup butter
1/3 cup milk
6 ounces chocolate chips
1 cup nuts, chopped

Mix cake mix as directed. Pour half of the batter into a greased 9x13-inch pan. Bake in preheated 350° oven for 15-20 minutes. Reduce heat to 250°. Melt caramels, butter, and milk together over low heat, stirring constantly. Pour over baked mixture. Sprinkle chocolate chips and nuts over top. Pour remaining cake batter over top of all and bake for 20 minutes at 250°, then 10 minutes more at 350°.

STEPHANIE'S BLUEBERRY BUCKLE

3/4 cup sugar
1/4 cup butter
1 egg
1/2 cup milk
1 cup flour
2 teaspoons baking powder
1/4 teaspoon salt

2 cups well-drained blueberries

Topping:
2/3 cup sugar
1/3 cup sifted flour
1/2 teaspoon cinnamon
1/3 cup melted butter

Mix sugar, butter, and egg thoroughly. Stir in milk. Sift together flour, baking powder, and salt. Add to egg mixture. Blend in blueberries. Spread batter into well prepared 8x12-inch pan. Mix topping ingredients together and sprinkle over batter. Bake at 375° for 35 to 40 minutes. May be served warm or cold. We prefer warm with ice cream!

Patiently waiting for dessert!

STRAWBERRY TORTE

1 cup butter
1 cup sugar
6 egg yolks
2 cups cake flour, sifted
1/2 teaspoon baking powder
1/2 teaspoon salt
6 egg whites
3/4 cup sugar
3 cups whipping cream
1 tablespoon sugar
1 teaspoon vanilla
1/2 cup currant jelly
1 cup coarsely chopped pecans
1 (12 ounce) jar strawberry jam

In large mixing bowl, cream butter and one cup sugar until very light and fluffy. Add eggs yolks, one at a time, beating well after each addition. Beat until fluffy and smooth, about five minutes. Sift flour, baking powder, and salt together. Stir into creamed mixture. Beat egg whites to soft peaks. Gradually add the 3/4 cup sugar, beating to stiff peaks. Fold into batter. Lightly grease bottoms of three 9-inch layer cake pans; pour in batter. Bake at 350° for 25-30 minutes. Cool. Beat the cream to stiff peaks and add one teaspoon each of sugar and vanilla. Spread the following mixtures over each cake layer:

<u>First layer</u> - Mix jelly with 1-cup whipped cream. Add 2-tablespoons nuts.
<u>Second layer</u> - Mix 2/3-cup jam, 1-cup whipped cream and 2-tablespoons nuts.
<u>Third layer</u> - Swirl remaining jam in 1-cup whipped cream.
<u>Sides</u> - Spread with 1/3-cup cream and remaining nuts.

We like to decorate this torte with ripe, red, and fresh Michigan strawberries. Place slices on the top of the cake or add a whole strawberry to individual servings.

TEXAS SHEET CAKE WITH FROSTING

1 cup butter
1 cup water
1/4 cup cocoa
2 cups sugar
2 cups flour
1/8 teaspoon salt
2 eggs
1 teaspoon baking soda
1/2 cup sour cream
1 teaspoon vanilla
3/4 cup chopped nuts (optional)

Combine butter, water, and cocoa in saucepan over medium heat until butter melts or heat in microwave until melted. Add sugar, flour, and salt, beating for one minute. Add eggs, soda, sour cream, and vanilla. Mix well. Fold in nuts. Pour into a 14x10x1-inch jelly roll pan. Bake at 350° for 20 minutes.

Frosting

1/2 cup butter
1/4 cup cocoa
1/4 cup plus 2 tablespoons milk
1 box powdered sugar, sifted
1/2 teaspoon vanilla
1/4 cup chopped nuts (optional)

Combine butter, cocoa, and milk in a saucepan. Bring to a boil. Add sugar and vanilla and beat with an electric mixer until blended. Spread on top of sheet cake and sprinkle with nuts.

This is one of our favorite dessert recipes for a crowd. The cake is very moist and can easily be served either in small squares on a buffet table, or in larger pieces on individual dessert plates. Sweet tip from Mom: serve it with vanilla ice cream for a mouthwatering combination!

COOKIES

The dining room is always bustling with activity, conversation, and fellowship during our evening meal. It's a great place to eat cookies, too!

APRICOT BARS
BROWN SUGAR WAFERS
BUTTERSCOTCH FUDGE BARS
BUTTERSCOTCH OATMEAL COOKIES
CHOCOLATE CHIP OATMEAL COOKIES
COCOA DROP COOKIES
DATE-ORANGE TOPPERS
EASY PEANUT BUTTER COOKIES
FUR TRADER COOKIES
GLENNY'S HEATH BITS PEANUT BUTTER COOKIES
GRANDMA'S ICE BOX COOKIES
GRANDMA'S SUGAR COOKIES
JAMBOREES
MINCEMEAT COOKIES
NO-BAKE COOKIES
NUT BUTTER BALLS
OATMEAL ICEBOX COOKIES
ORANGE BALLS – NO BAKE
PEANUT BUTTER BARS
PEANUT BUTTER COOKIES
PEANUT BUTTER LIGHT & CRUNCHY COOKIES
PEANUT BUTTER FUDGE
POLKA-DOT MACAROONS
POTATO CHIP COOKIES
PRALINE COOKIES
PUMPKIN CREAM CHEESE BARS
SEVEN-LAYER COOKIES
SO EASY CAKE MIX COOKIES

APRICOT BARS

Filling
1 heaping cup finely chopped dried apricots
1 cup water
2/3 cup sugar
1 teaspoon vanilla

Place apricots and water in covered pan and cook twenty minutes on medium-low heat. Add sugar and cook uncovered until thickened. Cool slightly; stir in vanilla. Cool completely.

Bars
2 cups soft butter
2 cups sugar
4 egg yolks
4 cups all-purpose flour
1 teaspoon salt
2 cups finely chopped pecans

Cream butter and sugar; add egg yolks and beat well. Stir in flour, salt, and pecans. Press 1/2 of mixture in 10x15 pan. Spread apricot filling on top, then spread remaining mixture over top of filling. Bake at 350° for approximately 50 minutes. Cool and cut into squares.

BROWN SUGAR WAFERS

1/2 pound butter – room temperature
1 box brown sugar
3 large eggs
2 teaspoons vanilla
2 cups sifted flour
1/2 teaspoon salt
1 cup chopped nutmeats

Preheat oven to 425°. Beat the butter and gradually add sugar, creaming thoroughly. Add eggs one at a time, beating after each. Add vanilla. Mix flour with salt and combine with nutmeats. Add to creamed mixture and mix well. Drop by teaspoonful onto greased baking sheet. Bake five to eight minutes or until edges are brown and crisp. Makes about forty.

BUTTERSCOTCH FUDGE BARS

These are really good and extremely easy to prepare!

1/2 cup butter
1 (1 ounce) envelope pre-melted unsweetened chocolate
1-1/2 cups all purpose flour
1/2 teaspoon baking soda
2 eggs
2 cups firmly packed brown sugar
1 teaspoon vanilla extract
3/4 cup chopped walnuts
Powdered sugar

Preheat oven to 350°. In large saucepan, melt butter and chocolate over low heat. Remove from heat and add remaining ingredients except powdered sugar. Blend well. Spread in prepared 9x13-inch pan and bake for 25 to 30 minutes. Cool, then sprinkle with powdered sugar. Cut into bars and enjoy!

BUTTERSCOTCH OATMEAL COOKIES

1 cup flour
1 teaspoon baking powder
1/2 teaspoon baking soda
1/2 teaspoon salt
1/2 cup butter, softened
3/4 cup brown sugar, firmly packed

1 large egg
1-1/2 teaspoons water
3/4 cup oatmeal
1 cup butterscotch morsels
1/4 teaspoon orange extract

Combine flour, baking powder, baking soda, and salt. Set aside. Combine and beat until creamy the butter, brown sugar, egg, and water. Gradually add the flour mixture to the creamed mixture. Fold in the oatmeal, butterscotch morsels, and orange extract until well mixed. Drop by teaspoonful onto greased baking sheet and bake at 375° for 10 to 12 minutes. Makes about thirty-six.

CHOCOLATE CHIP OATMEAL COOKIES

This recipe (our take on the Nestle Toll House Chocolate Chip Cookie recipe) is my husband's all-time favorite. We always make a double batch!

1 cup shortening
3/4 cup brown sugar
3/4 cup granulated sugar
1 teaspoon vanilla
2 eggs
1-1/4 cups flour

1-1/4 cups oatmeal
1 teaspoon baking soda
1 teaspoon salt
2 cups chocolate chips
Optional: 1 cup pecans, chopped

Beat butter, both sugars, and vanilla until creamy. Add eggs and beat well. Mix all flour, baking soda, and salt together and stir into batter a little at a time. Stir in chocolate chips and nuts. Bake at 375° for 9 to 11 minutes.

COCOA DROP COOKIES

1/2 cup shortening
1 cup sugar
1 egg
3/4 cup buttermilk
1 teaspoon vanilla

1-3/4 cups sifted flour
1/2 teaspoon soda
1/2 teaspoon salt
3 tablespoons cocoa
1/2 chopped pecans

Beat shortening, sugar, and egg together. Stir in buttermilk and vanilla. Sift dry ingredients together and stir in. Chill for at least one hour. Drop by teaspoonful onto a greased baking sheet. Bake at 400° for 8 to 10 minutes. Frost with a very thin layer of white icing.

<u>White Icing</u> – Make it thin for the Cocoa Drop Cookies
Beat together 4-tablespoons softened butter, 2-cups of powdered sugar, 1-teaspoon vanilla, and enough cream for easy spreading. This icing is great on cakes, too!

DATE – ORANGE TOPPERS

Cookie dough
1-2/3 cups flour
2 teaspoons baking powder
1/2 teaspoon salt
1/2 teaspoon nutmeg
1/2 teaspoon cinnamon
2/3 cup brown sugar, firmly packed
1/2 cup shortening
1 tablespoon cream or milk
1 egg
1 teaspoon vanilla extract
1 cup quick-cooking rolled oats

Date-Orange Filling
1/2 cup chopped candy orange slices
1/4 cup water
Dash of salt
1/2 cup chopped dates
1-1/2 teaspoons cornstarch
2 tablespoons water

Preheat oven to 375°. Combine all ingredients for cookie dough. Blend well with mixer. Shape into balls using a rounded teaspoon for each. Place onto ungreased cookie sheets. Combine orange slices, 1/4-cup water, salt, and dates in small saucepan. Cook over low heat until dates are soft, stirring occasionally. Combine cornstarch with 2-tablespoons water. Add to cooked mixture. Continue cooking and stirring until thick and clear. Cool. Form a hollow in center of each cookie with back of teaspoon. Place a teaspoon of the filling in the hollow. Bake for 12 to 15 minutes. Makes forty-two to forty-eight cookies.

EASY PEANUT BUTTER COOKIES

1 cup peanut butter, chunky or creamy
3/4 cup light brown sugar, packed
1 large egg
3/4 teaspoon baking soda

Heat oven to 350°. Beat all ingredients in a large bowl. Drop by level teaspoonful of dough onto prepared baking sheets. Bake until puffed and starting to lightly brown around edges, eight to ten minutes. Let cool on the baking sheet for five minutes, then transfer to a wire rack. Makes thirty-two cookies.

FUR TRADER COOKIES*

1 cup soft butter
1-1/2 cups sifted sugar
1 egg, lightly beaten
2-1/2 cups all-purpose flour
1 teaspoon cream of tartar
1 teaspoon salt
2 teaspoons baking powder
1 teaspoon nutmeg
2 tablespoons milk
1/4 teaspoon vanilla

Beat butter with sugar. Beat in egg. Sift dry ingredients together and add, alternately, with milk and vanilla. Mix well. Cover and chill one hour. Preheat oven to 375°. Using floured fingers, shape dough into balls. Place balls on baking sheet. Bake 12 to 15 minutes.

*Many years ago, the Fur Trader Cookies were served at the Fort Mackinac Tea Room. Robert Hughey (Little Bob), who operated the Fort Tea Room as a concession in 1971, sent this recipe to my mother-in-law, Jane Dunnigan. It's fun to bake and enjoy a taste of history!

GLENNY'S HEATH BITS PEANUT BUTTER COOKIES

1/2 cup shortening
3/4 cup creamy peanut butter
1-1/4 cups packed light brown sugar
3 tablespoons milk
1 tablespoon vanilla
1 egg

1-1/2 cups flour
3/4 teaspoon baking soda
3/4 teaspoon salt
1 (8 ounce) package Heath Milk Heath Toffee Bits

Preheat oven to 375°. Beat shortening, peanut butter, brown sugar, milk, and vanilla in large bowl until well blended. Add egg and beat just until blended. Combine flour, baking soda, and salt. Gradually beat into peanut butter mixture. Stir in 1-cup toffee bits. Drop by teaspoonful about two inches apart onto ungreased cookie sheet. Top each with reserved toffee bits. Bake 7 to 8 minutes or until set. Do not over bake. Cool two minutes. Remove to wire rack. Cool completely. Makes about three dozen.

This Ice Box Cookie recipe is one of Grandma Griffes' best loved recipes. She always served these cookies with a cup of hot and very strong coffee. So, of course, we became a family of cookie dunkers! Thanks, Grandma!

GRANDMA'S ICE BOX COOKIES

1 teaspoon baking soda
1/4 cup warm water
2 cups brown sugar
1 cup shortening

2 large eggs
1 teaspoon vanilla
4 cups flour
1 teaspoon cream of tarter
1 cup nutmeats

Dissolve baking soda in 1/4-cup warm water and set aside. Beat sugar and shortening together. Add eggs and vanilla and beat. Add soda and mix. Add flour, cream of tartar, and nutmeats. Mix well. Form a roll, chill, and then slice. Bake at 400° for 10 to 15 minutes. Makes about forty-eight cookies.

Grandma also made the BEST sugar cookies. We are carrying on the tradition; but for some reason, Grandma's tasted better!

GRANDMA'S SUGAR COOKIES

- 1 cup lard
- 2 cups sugar
- 2 eggs
- 2 teaspoons vanilla
- 1 teaspoon baking powder
- 1/4 teaspoon salt
- 4+ cups flour
- 1 teaspoon baking soda
- 1 cup sour milk
- Cherry jelly

Preheat oven to 350° and grease cookie sheets. Cream lard and sugar together. Add eggs and vanilla, beating well. Mix baking powder and salt with 4-cups flour. Stir baking soda into the sour milk. Gradually add moist and dry mixtures, alternately, until a soft dough is formed. Roll out onto a lightly-floured board and cut out cookies with a large round cutter. Using thumb, make indentation in middle of cookie. Fill indentation with cherry jelly. Bake 10 to 15 minutes, depending on size of cookie.

JAMBOREES

- 3 cups flour
- 1/2 teaspoon salt
- 1 cup sugar
- 1-1/4 cups butter, softened
- 1 tablespoon milk
- 2 eggs
- 2 tablespoons vanilla extract
- 1/2 cup apricot preserves
- 1/2 cup finely chopped walnuts

Combine all ingredients except preserves and walnuts. Blend well with mixer. Drop dough by teaspoonful onto ungreased baking sheets. Flatten with bottom of glass dipped in sugar. Spoon 1/4-teaspoon preserves into center of cookie and sprinkle with walnuts. Bake at 375° for 10 to 12 minutes until lightly browned.

MINCEMEAT COOKIES

3/4 cup shortening
1-1/2 cups sugar
3 eggs, well beaten
1 teaspoon baking soda
3 cups all purpose flour
3/4 teaspoon salt
1 (9 ounce) package mincemeat
3 tablespoons water
1 cup nutmeats, broken

Cream shortening and sugar together. Add eggs and beat well. Stir in one half of the sifted dry ingredients. Add finely crumbled mincemeat and water; stir until blended. Add nutmeats and remaining flour mixture. Mix well. Drop by teaspoonful onto greased baking sheet. Bake at 350° for 10-15 minutes. Makes about forty-eight cookies.

NO-BAKE COOKIES

2 cups sugar
3 tablespoons cocoa
1/2 cup milk
Pinch of salt
1/4 pound butter
3 cups quick-cooking oatmeal
1/2 cup peanut butter
1 teaspoon vanilla

Mix sugar, cocoa, milk, salt, and butter in a saucepan. Bring to boiling point and boil for one full minute. Mix in oatmeal, peanut butter, and vanilla. Drop cookies by teaspoonful onto cookie sheet and let cool. They are ready to eat when cold. Makes thirty-six cookies.

We started making No-Bake Cookies when I was a Girl Scout in elementary school. My friends and I would make double batches to take on camping trips. My mother and the other leaders never seemed to mind our sugar highs! Because these are easy to make and delightfully tasty, they are a staple at the cottage every year.

NUT BUTTER BALLS

2 cups sifted all-purpose flour
1/4 cup sugar
1/2 teaspoon salt
1 cup butter
2 teaspoons vanilla
2 cups chopped pecans
Powdered sugar

Preheat oven to 350°. Sift flour, sugar, and salt. Work in butter and vanilla. Add nuts, mix well. Shape in small bite-size balls and place onto greased baking sheet. Bake 40 minutes then roll in powdered sugar while warm. Makes about forty-five cookies.

Nut Butter Balls have been my favorite since I was a small child. Mom was a fabulous cookie baker and she still holds that title!
My brother David and sister Cheryl had their favorites, too. Oatmeal Ice-Box was just one!

OATMEAL ICEBOX COOKIES

1 cup shortening
1 cup brown sugar
1 cup sugar
2 eggs
1 teaspoon vanilla
3 cups long-cooking oatmeal
1 teaspoon salt
1 teaspoon baking soda
1-1/2 cups all-purpose flour
1/2 cup walnut nutmeats

Cream shortening and sugars. Add eggs and vanilla. Mix dry ingredients together and stir into creamed mixture. Fold in nuts. Mix into roll and refrigerator for several hours. Slice and bake at 400° for 10-15 minutes. Do not flour board as dough is dry enough to roll. Makes approximately three-dozen cookies.

ORANGE BALLS – NO BAKE

1 (13 ounce) box vanilla wafers, crushed
1 (6 ounce) can frozen orange juice
1/4 pound butter
2 cups powdered sugar
Shredded coconut

Combine first four ingredients and make into small balls. Roll the balls in coconut. Refrigerate overnight. Makes three-dozen balls. They freeze well.

PEANUT BUTTER BARS

1 cup white sugar
1 cup white syrup
2 cups peanut butter
2 cups corn flakes
2 cups Rice Krispies
4 tablespoons butter
2 tablespoons cocoa (or more)
3 tablespoons milk
Powdered sugar

Peanut Butter Bars are delicious and definitely a cottage favorite! We frequently take these to Island events when we are asked to bring a sweet treat. There is never anything left but an empty plate. NEVER!

Boil sugar and syrup until sugar dissolves. Add peanut butter and mix well. Stir in cereals and spread evenly in a 9x13-inch pan. Heat butter and cocoa to dissolve, and then add milk and enough powdered sugar to make a spreading consistency. Spread the frosting over the cooled bars. Cut into bars and enjoy!

This recipe was given to all docents who served at the Governor's Summer Residence by former Governor Jennifer Granholm. This beautiful Mackinac Island summer residence is open to the public for tours every Wednesday morning during the summer season.

PEANUT BUTTER COOKIES

9 ounces butter
6 ounces brown sugar
6 ounces sugar
1/4 teaspoon salt

9 ounces peanut butter
3 ounces eggs
12 ounces pastry flour
1/4 teaspoon baking soda

Method: Cream together the butter, both sugars, salt, and peanut butter. Add eggs slowly. Add sifted flour and baking soda, mix. Pan and bake at 375 degrees. Cool cookies completely in the cooler. Melt 2 cups melting chocolate with 2 tablespoons of shortening over a double-boiler. Dip cookies 1/2 in chocolate and cool.

PEANUT BUTTER LIGHT & CRUNCHY COOKIES – *Our favorite!*

1 cup shortening
1 cup peanut butter
1 cup sugar
1 cup powdered sugar
2 large eggs

1 teaspoon vanilla
2 cups all-purpose flour
2 teaspoons baking soda
1 teaspoon salt

Cream shortening, peanut butter, and sugars. Add eggs and vanilla. Beat well. Sift flour, soda, and salt together. Gradually add to other ingredients. Drop by teaspoonful onto ungreased baking sheet. Lightly dipping into flour with fork, make crisscross marks on each cookie. Bake 350° for 15 to 20 minutes. Makes thirty-six to forty-eight cookies.

It is impossible to eat just one of these light, melt-in-your-mouth cookies! Guaranteed!

PEANUT BUTTER FUDGE – *Barbara's best!*

3 tablespoons butter plus enough for coating saucepan
3 cups sugar
1/8 teaspoon salt
1-1/2 cups whole milk
3 heaping tablespoons peanut butter
1 teaspoon vanilla

Lightly coat bottom and sides of saucepan with butter. Combine sugar, salt, and milk. Cook over medium-high heat, stirring until it comes to a boil. Continue cooking to a soft ball stage, 235°. Remove from heat. Add butter, peanut butter, and vanilla to the pan, but do not stir until mixture cools slightly, about 110°. Beat the mixture and turn into a buttered pan.

Mom's tip for fudge: peanut butter fudge can make fabulous frosting for a cake, yellow or chocolate. All you have to do is cook the fudge to a little less than the soft-ball stage so that it will spread nicely.

Mom's tip number two for fudge: stop at one of the famous Mackinac Island fudge shops and it will keep you out of the kitchen!

Thanks, Mom!

POLKA-DOT MACAROONS

5 cups flaked coconut
1 can sweetened condensed milk
1/2 cup all-purpose flour
1-1/2 cups M&M miniature baking bits

In a large bowl, combine the coconut, milk, and flour. Stir in baking bits. Drop by rounded teaspoonful, two inches apart, onto baking sheets coated with cooking spray. Bake 350° for eight to ten minutes or until edges are lightly browned. Remove to wire racks. Makes approximately 4-1/2 dozen.

There's nothing like a good cookie or two to celebrate a long stroll. Whether walking around the Island, to Arch Rock, or even downtown along the boardwalk, it's always nice to know that a homemade cookie awaits you upon your return!

POTATO CHIP COOKIES – *sweet and salty!*

1/2 cup sugar
2 cups all-purpose flour
1/2 cup potato chips, crunched
1 teaspoon vanilla
1/2 cup chopped pecans
2 cups butter

Mix all ingredients together. Roll into balls and flatten. Sprinkle with sugar. Bake at 375° for ten minutes. Makes thirty-six.

PRALINE COOKIES

1 cup condensed milk
2/3 cup brown sugar
6 tablespoons melted butter
2 cups nutmeats

2 eggs
1/2 cup sifted flour
1/4 teaspoon maple flavoring

Cook milk and sugar in a double boiler until very thick. Remove from heat and stir in melted butter and nuts. Cool slightly. Beat eggs and add to mixture. Blend in flour. Stir in maple flavoring. Drop by teaspoonful onto a baking sheet. Bake about 12 minutes at 350° until lightly browned.

PUMPKIN CREAM CHEESE BARS

1-1/4 cups flour
3/4 cup sugar, divided
1/2 cup packed brown sugar
3/4 cup cold butter, cubed
1 cup old-fashioned oatmeal
1/2 cup pecan pieces
8 ounces cream cheese, softened
2 teaspoons cinnamon
1 teaspoon allspice
1 teaspoon cardamom
1 (15 ounce) can pumpkin
1 teaspoon vanilla
3 eggs, beaten

Heat oven to 350° and spray a 9x13-inch metal baking pan. In a small bowl, mix flour, 1/4-cup of sugar, and the brown sugar. Cut in butter until crumbly. Stir in oats and pecans. Press crumb mixture into prepared pan reserving one cup for topping. Bake for 15 minutes.

Meanwhile, in a small bowl, beat cream cheese, spices, and remaining white sugar until smooth. Beat in pumpkin and vanilla. Add eggs and beat on low speed until just blended. Pour over warm crust and sprinkle with reserved crumb mixture. Bake for 20-25 minutes until bars test clean. Cool on a wire rack. Serve immediately, or refrigerate within two hours.

SEVEN-LAYER COOKIES

8 ounces margarine
1 cup graham cracker crumbs
6 ounces chocolate chips
6 ounces butterscotch chips
1 cup condensed milk
1 cup coconut
1 cup nutmeats, chopped

Melt margarine in 8x12-inch pan in oven. Layer graham cracker crumbs, chocolate chips, and butterscotch chips. Pour condensed milk over all. Sprinkle coconut and nutmeats on top. Bake 30 minutes at 350°. Cut in squares when cool.

SO EASY CAKE MIX COOKIES – *made your way! Thanks Bev!*

Use your imagination to create your very own special family favorite cookie. Select any flavor boxed cake mix and your favorite two extra ingredients.

1 package cake mix – flavor of your choice
2 large eggs
1 cup vegetable oil
EXTRA INGREDIENT - 1 cup of an extra ingredient such as chopped nuts
EXTRA INGREDIENT - 1 cup of another ingredient such as chocolate chips

With an electric mixer, beat the cake mix, eggs, and oil until batter thickens. Add extra ingredients. Drop by teaspoonful onto prepared baking sheet. Bake at 350° for 15 to 20 minutes. Makes about thirty-six.

Mom recently used a chocolate cake mix and added chocolate chips and pecans. Another time she used a lemon cake mix and added white chocolate pieces and walnuts.

The **Mackinac Island Cottage Cookbook** is a collection of some of our favorite recipes. Several are original, but most of them have been shared with us by visiting family and friends. Over the years, these recipes have been tossed into a wire basket on "Granny's cupboard" in our cottage kitchen. Eventually, Mom took them all to her home in Florida, organized them, placed them in a notebook, and named it "Donnybrook Cookbook". More recipes were added every summer, and then one day Mom said, "Let's write a cookbook to reflect the love of family, friends, and happy times using these recipes." And so, we did just that. Now, along with Mom's sister, my Aunt Sharon, we are excited to share this "labor of love" with you. We hope you will enjoy each page of the book as much as we have enjoyed writing it.

Barbara Toms   Marcia Dunnigan

Thank you to all of our family and friends who have inspired us with their favorite recipes and motivated us during our writing adventure. We are blessed to be able to spend special moments and make Mackinac memories with you.

We wish to express our heartfelt gratitude to my husband Dan who has shared ideas and given unwavering support and encouragement to our efforts. Of course, he is our on-site taste-tester as well! Also, extra kudos to Janet Meerpohl who stepped in to help with editing.

Although both Barbara Toms and Marcia Dunnigan are native Michiganders, they now winter in Naples, Florida. Barbara enjoys shows, movies, church activities, just hanging out, and spur-of-the moment shopping with her daughter. Marcia lives with her husband Dan and loves visiting with their three daughters, playing with their grandson, walking the beach, traveling, entertaining, and playing bridge, especially with her favorite partner, Mom!

Sharon Griffes Tarr

As an artist....

I have been truly blessed to intimately experience Mackinac Island for many years and share in the love of family at Donnybrook Cottage. Hiking and biking the Island with sketchpad and paints is part of my daily ritual during summertime visits. My day usually begins early before the first boat from the mainland arrives. It is this special time of day when I love to explore and capture the Island's natural beauty. Later, as the day blooms, I am drawn to the activities of the Island people, its visitors, and animals.

You will find a multitude of my Island watercolor sketches and oil paintings created over a number of years in this book. The back-cover painting depicts the view as seen from Donnybrook Cottage at sunset. I hope these sketches and paintings help give you a visual taste of Mackinac Island's natural beauty.

Formal art training began in my teens with artist, Leland Beeman at Stone Village in Jackson, Michigan and continued at the American Academy of Art in Chicago. I also studied with several living masters including: Chen Khee Chee, Albert Handel, and Marc Hanson. My current work has been largely influenced by the great Fred Cuming, RA of England, and America's past master John Singer Sargent.

Today, my working studio is located near Williamston, Michigan where I live with my husband Paul M. Tarr, Jr. A busy teaching schedule includes local and regionally conducted studio classes and workshops. My current work may be viewed at several galleries which represent me and on my website at *www.SGTarr.com*.

INDEX

APPETIZERS AND HORS D'OEURVES

Appetizer Pie, 4
Baguette Toasts, 7
Brie Appetizer, 8
Brie with Strawberry Jam, 9
Cheese - Sausage Bites, 10
Cheesy Corn Bites, 10
Cheryl's Baked Brie, 9
Chicken Salad Tea Sandwiches, 11
Chili-Cranberry Meatballs, 12
Cranberry-Rum Brie, 8
Diane's Dill Bits, 14
Finger Jell-O, 15
Ham & Cheese Roll-ups, 16
Herb-coated Mozzarella, 16
Mexican Fudge, 19
Mini Ham and Cheese Sandwiches, 20
Mini Turkey Sandwiches, 21
Mock Boursin Cheese, 21
Mushrooms, 22
Onion Rye Appetizers, 23
Pimiento Cheese Ball, 23
Pinwheels, 24
Roka Cheese Roll, 24
Roquefort Grapes, 25
Smoked Salmon Roll-ups, 26
Spinach Roll-ups, 27
Sriracha Wings, 28
Stuffed Celery, 28
Stuffed Dates, 29
Taco Appetizer, 29
Three-Layer Cheese Torte, 31
Veggie Pizza, 32
Wonton Wrappers with Salami, 32

Dips and Spreads

Artichoke & Cheese Spread, 6
Artichoke & Spinach Dip, 5
Artichoke Dip, 4
Artichoke Dip – Florentine, 5
Baked Apricot Spread, 7
Blue Cheese Dip, 7
Chili Con Queso, 11
Chili Pimiento Cheese Spread, 12
Clam Dip, 12
Curry Dip, 13
Easy Crab Spread, 14
Feta Salsa, 15
Guacamole Dip, 15
Hot Bean Dip, 17
Hot Crab Dip, 17
Jeanne's Avocado Dip, 18
Jeb's Favorite Shrimp Dip, 19
Mex-Tex Refried Beans Dip, 20
Mustard Dip, 22
Seven-Layer Fiesta Dip, 25
Smoked Whitefish Spread, 26
Southwestern Shrimp Dip in Lettuce Bowl, 27
Taco Dip, 30
Vegetable Cheese Dip, 31
Veggie Dip, 32

BEEF

Basic Brisket, 87
Corned Beef Casserole, 140
Country-Style Pot Roast, 88
Crazy Beef Stew, 88
Cubed Steak Parmigianino, 89
Easy Beef Burgundy, 90
Ellen's Eye of Round, 91
Five Layer Casserole, 92
Flank Steak, 92
Jill's Chili Rellenos, 94
Marinara & Meatballs, 142
Mil's Meat Loaf - Pot Roast Style, 94
My Favorite Beef Stew, 95
Oven Beef Burgundy, 96
Overnight Pot Roast, 97
Peggy's Shredded Beef, 98
Pot Roast, 100
Sloppy Joes, 101
Slow-cooked Brisket, 102
Steak with Blue Cheese Spread, 102
Whole Beef Tenderloin - Oven Roasted, 102

BREADS AND COFFEE CAKES
Bea's Mondel Bread, *35*
Cherry Swirl Coffee Cake, *36*
Cinnamon Rolls, *36*
Monkey Bread, *37*
Orange Nut Bread, *37*
Pull-a-part Bread, *38*
Pumpkin Bread, *39*
Quick Cheese & Garlic Bread, *39*
Salty Bread Sticks, *40*
Six-Weeks Bran Muffins, *40*
Sour Cream Coffee Cake, *41*
Zombie Bread, *42*
Zucchini Walnut Bread, *42*

BREAKFAST/BRUNCH DISHES
Bacon, Egg, & Tomato Strata, *45*
Banana Cream Crumble French Toast, *46*
Basic Quiche, *47*
Breakfast Crockpot Casserole, *47*
Breakfast Muffins, *48*
Brunch Enchiladas, *49*
Brunch Fruit Cup, *49*
Chris's Easy Cheese Soufflé, *50*
Green Chile Brunch Bake, *50*
Hot Fruit, *51*
Huevos Ranchero, *51*
Overnight French Toast Casserole with Strawberries, *52*
Spinach, Bacon, & Mushroom Quiche, *53*
Theo's Toast with Avocado & Fresh Tomato, *53*
Tomato Florentine Quiche, *54*
Vivian's Cottage Cheese Pancakes, *54*

CAKES AND TORTES
Apple Cake with Glace, *175*
Barbie's Butterscotch Chocolate Cake, *178*
Brownie Refrigerator Cake, *179*
Coca-Cola Cake, *181*
Cranberry Pound Cake with Hot Caramel Sauce, *182*
Gingerbread Cake, *185*
Glorious Dump Cake, *185*
Heavenly Orange-Pineapple Cake, *186*
Kahlúa Chocolate Cake, *189*
Lemon Cake, *191*
Lush Lemon Frosting, *192*
Peanut Butter Fudge for Frosting, *218*
Pineapple Angel Food Cake, *194*
Pineapple Fruit Cake, *195*
Pumpkin Pie Cake, *198*
Rocky's Caramel Cake, *200*
Strawberry Torte, *201*
Texas Sheet Cake with Frosting, *202*

COOKIES AND BARS
Apricot Bars, *205*
Brown Sugar Wafers, *206*
Butterscotch Fudge Bars, *206*
Butterscotch Oatmeal Cookies, *207*
Chocolate Chip Oatmeal Cookies, *208*
Cocoa Drop Cookies, *208*
Date-Orange Toppers, *209*
Easy Peanut Butter Cookies, *210*
Fur Trader Cookies, *210*
Grandma's Sugar Cookies, *213*
Glenny's Heath Bits Peanut Butter Cookies, *211*
Grandma's Ice Box Cookies, *212*
Jamborees, *213*
Mincemeat Drop Cookies, *214*
No-Bake Cookies, *214*
Nut Butter Balls, *215*
Oatmeal Ice Box Cookies, *215*
Orange Balls - No Bake, *216*
Peanut Butter Bars, *216*
Peanut Butter Cookies, *217*
Peanut Butter Fudge, *218*
Peanut Butter Light & Crunchy Cookies, *217*
Polka-Dot Macaroons, *219*
Potato Chip Cookies, *219*
Praline Cookies, *220*
Pumpkin Cream Cheese Bars, *221*
Seven-Layer Cookies, *221*
So Easy Cake Mix Cookies, *222*

DESSERTS AND SAUCES
Apple & Cranberry Crisp, 175
Apple Pie with Salted Caramel, 476
Banana & Strawberry Trifle, 178
Banana Split Dessert, 177
Cherry Pie, 179
Chocolate Heath Trifle, 180
East Bluff Strawberry Shortcake, 183
Frozen Pumpkin Ice Cream Pie, 184
Hot Fudge Sauce, 186
Ice Cream Pie with Caramel Sauce, 187
Jo's Dessert, 188
Key Lime Pie, 189
Lemon Delight, 191
Lemon Sauce, 192
Lemonade Cheesecake, 190
Peach Dumplings, 193
Peanut Butter Pie (Easy), 193
Pie Crust, 194
Pumpkin Chiffon, 195
Pumpkin Dessert, 197
Pumpkin Pie, 197
Pumpkin Pie - Turtle Style, 198
Rhubarb Crisp, 199
Stephanie's Blueberry Buckle, 200

MARINADES
Blue Cheese Spread for Steak, 102
Key Lime Marinade, 120
Lemon-Basil Marinade, 120
The Only Marinade You'll Ever Need, 104
The Perfect Rub, 104

PASTA
Baked or Grilled Chicken with Angel Hair Pasta, 135
Baked Turkey Ziti, 135
Cavatappi with Grilled Chicken & Asparagus, 136
Chicken & Broccoli Alfredo, 137
Chicken Lasagna, 138
Chicken Pasta Parmesan, 139
Chicken Tetrazzini, 140
Corned Beef Casserole, 140
Creamy Chicken Alfredo, 113
Creamy Clam Spaghetti, 141
Easy Beef Burgundy, 90
Easy Lasagna, 141
Zesty Parmesan Pasta, 150
Grandma's Macaroni and Cheese, 143
Marinara & Meatballs, 142
Parmesan Linguini, 144
Sausage & Macaroni Casserole, 145
Seafood Lasagna, 146
Shrimp Scampi, 147
Shrimp Thermidor, 148
So Easy Fresh Tomato Sauce, 149
Spaghetti Carbonara, 149
Veggie Lasagna, 150
Zesty Parmesan Pasta, 150

PORK
Coca-Cola Ribs, 87
Fay's Bourbon Pork Tenderloin, 91
Garlic Roast Pork with Sun-Dried Tomatoes, 93
Pork Patties with Mandarin Sauce, 98
Pork Roast, 99
Pork Stir Fry with Peaches, 99
Pork Tenderloin with Maple Mustard Sauce, 100
Pulled Pork, 101
Sausage & Macaroni Casserole, 145

POTATOES
Flying High Mashed Potatoes, 160
Four-Cheese Scalloped Potatoes, 161
Parmesan Mashed Potatoes, 164
Potatoes Supreme, 165
Roasted Potatoes & Veggies, 166
Scalloped Potatoes, 167
Sweet Potato Casserole, 168
Sweet Potatoes with Apples, 169

POULTRY

Apricot-Lime Chicken Thighs, *107*
Baked or Grilled Chicken with Angel Hair Pasta, *135*
Baked Turkey Ziti, *135*
Cavatappi with Grilled Chicken & Asparagus, *136*
Chicken and Broccoli Alfredo, *137*
Chicken Cheddar Bake, *107*
Chicken Dressing Bake, *108*
Chicken Lasagna, *138*
Chicken Pasta Parmesan, *139*
Chicken Patties Mandarin, *109*
Chicken Piccata, *110*
Chicken Pie in English Pastry, *111*
Chicken Tetrazzini, *140*
Chicken with Artichoke/Mushrooms, *112*
Chicken with Cheese, *112*
Creamy Chicken Alfredo, *113*
Creamy Chicken Enchiladas, *114*
Crispy Baked Chicken, *115*
Crunchy Onion Chicken, *115*
Easy Baked Chicken, *115*
Panko Encrusted Chicken Breasts, *116*
Ritz Cracker Chicken, *117*
Sandy's Honey Mustard Chicken, *117*
Simple Coca-Cola Chicken, *117*
Tarragon Chicken, *118*
Trish's Chicken Roll-ups, *118*

SALADS

Bacon, Tomato, & Potato Salad, *67*
Broccoli Salad, *68*
Broccoli & Creamy Feta Salad, *68*
Buffet Salad, *69*
Chicken Salad, *69*
Chicken Salad for six or thirty, *70*
Corned Beef Salad, *71*
Crunchy Pea Salad, *71*
Cucumbers in Sour Cream, *72*
Easy Shrimp Salad, *72*
Fresh Spinach Salad, *73*
Jell-O Ribbon Salad, *73*
Layered Cobb Salad, *74*
Layered Spinach Salad, *75*
Macaroni Salad, *75*
Marcia's Salad, *76*
Seven Layer Salad, *76*
Shrimp Salad, *77*
Spinach Salad with Blue Cheese, *77*
Spinach Tarragon Salad, *78*
Taco Salad, *79*
Taco Salad - Jill's Easy & Tasty, *79*

Dressings
Celery Seed Dressing, *80*
Chunky Blue Cheese Dressing, *81*
Fruit Salad Dressing, *81*
Fruit Salad Lime Dressing, *81*
Janet's Dressing, *82*
Katie's Bacon Dressing, *83*
Nancy's Vinaigrette, *83*
Peach Fruit Dressing, *84*
Southwest Dressing, *84*
Thousand Island Dressing, *84*

SANDWICHES

Chicken Salad Tea Sandwiches, *11*
Mini Ham & Cheese Sandwiches, *20*
Mini Turkey Sandwiches, *21*
Peggy's Shredded Beef, *98*
Pulled Pork, *101*
Sandy's Shrimp Toast, *128*
Sloppy Joes, *101*
Toast with Avocado & Fresh Tomato, *53*
Tuna Sandwiches, *132*

SEAFOOD

Baked Lake Michigan White Fish or Michigan Trout, *123*
Barbara's Fried Perch, *123*
Creamy Clam Spaghetti, *141*
Eric's Kickin' Shrimp, *124*
Fabulous Shrimp, *125*
Fillet of Sole with Mushrooms, *125*
Herb-Glazed Salmon, *125*

Martha's Famous Fish Tacos, *126*
Mustard-Dill Baked Salmon, *127*
Sandy's Shrimp Toast, *128*
Seafood Lasagna, *146*
Seafood Quiche, *128*
Sesame Ginger Salmon, *129*
Shrimp Scampi, *147*
Shrimp Thermidor, *148*
Slow-Roasted Lemon-Ginger Salmon, *130*
Stuffed Sole, *131*
Tilapia Dijon, *132*
Tuna Sandwiches, *132*

SIDE DISHES
Addy's Marvelous Mushrooms, *153*
Alsatian Onion Tart, *154*
Asparagus & Blue Cheese, *155*
Asparagus Bundles, *156*
Asparagus with Tomatoes, *156*
Baked Pineapple, *157*
Brussels Sprouts, *157*
Cheese-Frosted Cauliflower, *158*
Cheesy Broccoli Casserole, *158*
Corn Spoon Bread, *159*
Cowboy Slow Cooker Beans, *159*
Flying High Mashed Potatoes, *160*
Four-Cheese Scalloped Potatoes, *161*
Garlic-Toasted Asparagus, *162*
Grandma's Macaroni and Cheese, *143*
Green Beans & Portobello Mushroom Sauté, *163*
Green Beans with Browned Butter, *163*
Old English Asparagus Casserole, *164*
Parmesan Linguini, *144*
Parmesan Mashed Potatoes, *164*
Potatoes Supreme, *165*
Roasted Potatoes & Veggies, *166*
Sausage Stuffing Balls, *166*
Roasted Brussels Sprouts with Pancetta & Sage, *165*
Scalloped Potatoes, *167*
Spinach & Mushroom Casserole, *168*
Squash Soufflé, *170*

Sweet Potato Casserole, *168*
Sweet Potatoes with Apples, *169*
Veggie Casserole, *170*
White Mold, *171*
Zesty Parmesan Pasta, *150*
Zucchini Au Gratin, *172*
Zucchini Casserole, *172*

SOUPS
Beach-Bar Tomato Soup, *57*
Bean & Ham Soup, *58*
Broccoli Cheese Soup, *58*
Broccoli, White Bean, and Cheddar Soup, *59*
Creamy Tomato Soup, *59*
Easy Turkey Chili, *60*
Gazpacho, *60*
Max's Onion Soup, *61*
Ohio Chili, *61*
Roasted Cauliflower Soup, *62*
Sharel's Strawberry Soup, *62*
Turkey Chili, *63*
Vichyssoise, *63*
Watercress Soup, *64*
White Bean Chili, *64*

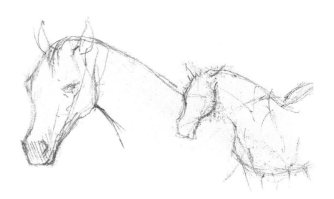